Accounting Demystified

Accounting Demystified

Jeffry R. Haber, Ph.D., CPA

AMACOM

American Management Association

New York • Atlanta • Brussels • Chicago • Mexico City • San Francisco
Shanghai • Tokyo • Toronto • Washington, D.C.

Special discounts on bulk quantities of AMACOM books are available to corporations, professional associations, and other organizations. For details, contact Special Sales Department, AMACOM, a division of American Management Association, 1601 Broadway, New York, NY 10019.
Tel.: 212-903-8316. Fax: 212-903-8083.
Web site: www.amacombooks.org

Library of Congress Cataloging-in-Publication Data

Haber, Jeffry R., 1960–
    Accounting demystified / Jeffry R. Haber.
      p. cm.
   ISBN 978-0-8144-0790-5
   1. Accounting. I. Title.

  HF5635.H112   2004
  657—dc22

                       2003017265

Printing number

10 9 8 7 6 5 4 3 2 1

Contents

Acknowledgments

I would like to thank my wonderful wife, Holly, and the greatest group of children any father could be blessed with: Jonathan, Amy, and Lauren. They were extremely understanding during the process of writing this book.

I would also like to thank the team at AMACOM, especially Ray O'Connell and Jim Bessent, who made the development of this book painless.

Finally, I would like to thank you, the reader, for your interest in financial accounting, without which this book would not be necessary.

Accounting
Demystified

1

Introduction

The success or failure of a business is measured in dollars. And dollars are recorded and reported using accounting. Accounting is truly the language of business. No matter what your role may be, if you are involved in business, you can benefit from learning accounting. That's what this book is all about—taking the subject and making it understandable and accessible.

This book makes an excellent companion to any standard text, or it can be used as a stand-alone volume. It is designed to present the subject in a straightforward, approachable manner. Financial accounting is an incremental process. What you learn in earlier chapters is used in later ones. There are no shortcuts to learning financial accounting, but at the same time, if it is taught clearly, it is not difficult.

Financial accounting involves all the steps from the original entries in the accounting records to the preparation of financial statements. There are other types of accounting as well, such as managerial accounting, cost accounting, and tax accounting, to name a few. These other types of accounting are covered in other books. The end user of financial accounting is the public; therefore, financial accounting has a lot of rules. These rules are necessary to make the information presented in the financial statements consistent and understandable. In contrast, in managerial accounting, which is used by the managers of a business to improve the business's operations, efficiency, and profitability, there are relatively few rules. Instead, it primarily consists of techniques that have proved themselves over time.

The organization of this book is intended to present the material in the order in which it needs to be understood. Therefore, we start with the end product of financial accounting, the financial statements, then jump back to the first step in the accounting process, making journal entries. This may seem out of order, but it follows the way accounting is best understood and learned rather than following the chronology of how accounting is done.

You cannot be a good accountant if you are not a good bookkeeper. Bookkeeping is considered a lower-level profession than accounting, and this perception is accurate because accountants possess skills that bookkeepers do not. However, the first step in learning accounting is to learn bookkeeping. What makes it accounting and not simply bookkeeping is going beyond just recording the entries into such areas as preparing the financial statements, analyzing the statements, and making necessary adjusting entries at the end of the accounting period.

A last thing to keep in mind when reading this book and looking at the examples and descriptions is that how things are presented and how they are arranged are highly variable in practice. Companies and managers adapt forms, schedules, and statements to meet their own needs (within the existing rules). Except as specifically prescribed by accounting guidance, there is an abundance of flexibility. A nimble mind will come in handy in trying to reconcile what is described in this book with what you may see in the real world. Sometimes these will be the same and sometimes there will be minor differences in presentation, but even given that variability, it should not be hard to take what you learn from this book and relate it directly to real-world situations.

CHAPTER 2

Financial Statements

The end product of the financial accounting process is the financial statements. There are four basic financial statements: the Balance Sheet, the Income Statement, the Statement of Retained Earnings, and the Statement of Cash Flows. In addition to the four financial statements there will also be a section called "notes to the financial statements" or "footnotes." This section provides additional information that helps the reader understand certain details without making the basic statements overly long.

Sometimes the basic financial statements will have slightly different names, such as the Statement of Income instead of the Income Statement or the Statement of Changes in Owner's Equity instead of the Statement of Retained Earnings. Accountants have flexibility when it comes to account titles and statement names; the important thing is that anyone can recognize what the account or statement is. The names and titles used in this book are both typical and descriptive.

Income Statement

The Income Statement lists the company's revenues and expenses and gives the difference between them. This difference is called *net income*. For the most part, revenues arise from selling goods or services. Expenses are the costs involved in operating the business.

Some examples of accounts that are classified as revenues and expenses are:

Revenues	Expenses
Sales	Cost of goods sold
Interest income	Salary expense
	Rent expense
	Tax expense
	Interest expense

This is a very short list of the accounts that may be found on the Income Statement. Salary expense is also known as Wage expense or Payroll expense. The names are synonymous and are used interchangeably. It is also common not to use the full title Rent expense, but to call it simply Rent. This is done for most items where there is not a revenue and an expense with similar names. For instance, in the list given here, we cannot call Interest income simply Interest, since if we did, we would not be able to distinguish between the income and expense accounts. We have to use the full name Interest income in order not to confuse this account with Interest expense. When an account comes in two flavors (income and expense), we cannot shorten its name.

The Income Statement is concerned with how much

money the company brought in and how much it spent in order to bring that money in. The Income Statement covers a period of time. This period may be a month, a quarter, six months, a year, or any other period of time that the company feels is appropriate. Many companies prepare their financial statements on a monthly, quarterly, and annual basis. A proper heading for the Income Statement will have three lines: the name of the company, the name of the statement, and the period of time the statement covers. An example is:

Jeffry Haber Company
Income Statement
For the Year Ended December 31, 2002

If the statement is for the quarter ended December 31, 2002, there are two acceptable ways to state the period of time:

For the Quarter Ended December 31, 2002

For the Three Months Ended December 31, 2002

The revenues are listed in one section and the expenses in another. The order of the accounts within each section is usually determined by the size of the account balances, with the largest balances listed first. Each section is then totaled.

Financial statements have some weird rules. For one thing, it is typical to capitalize only the first letter of each account name (for example, Interest income). There are also some other peculiarities related to the appearance of the financial statements. The first number in each section gets a dollar sign ($), as does the last number in each section. The last number before a subtotal is underlined, and the final total is double-underlined. Each number in a section is indented after the subheading. Figure 2-1 is an example of a typical Income Statement.

Even though such rules seem silly, and for the most part are not very important as long as it is obvious to the reader how to interpret the information, they do serve a purpose. The double underline tells the reader what the final total of the statement is. The single underline alerts the reader that a sub-total is coming on the next line. Indenting is an efficient way of depicting a grouping of like items.

Statement of Retained Earnings

The Statement of Retained Earnings takes the beginning balance of Retained earnings (which is the same as the ending

---

FIGURE 2-1

Jeffry Haber Company
Income Statement
For the Year Ended December 31, 2002

Revenues:	
Sales	$250,000
Interest income	500
Total revenue	$250,500
Expenses:	
Payroll	$125,000
Payroll taxes	20,000
Rent	10,000
Telephone	7,000
Office supplies	3,000
Total expenses	$165,000
Net income	$ 85,500

balance from the previous period), then adds net income and subtracts dividends paid to stockholders to arrive at the ending balance of Retained earnings. Dividends are distributions of money to shareholders. The Statement of Retained Earnings is for a period of time, and the period should be the same as that of the Income Statement. A dollar sign ($) is used for the first and last numbers, and the last number is double-underlined. Some people like to use a subtotal after net income, but this is not required.

A sample Statement of Retained Earnings is given in Figure 2-2.

Note that the net income amount is the same as the net income shown on the Income Statement. The financial statements are related to one another, and at times, a figure from one statement is carried over to another statement.

Balance Sheet

The Balance Sheet lists the assets, liabilities, and equity accounts of the company. The Balance Sheet is prepared "as on" a particular day, and the accounts reflect the balances that existed at the close of business on that day. The Balance Sheet is

---

FIGURE 2-2

Jeffry Haber Company
Statement of Retained Earnings
For the Year Ended December 31, 2002

Beginning balance, January 1, 2002	$100,000
Add: Net income	85,500
Less: Dividends	35,500
Ending balance, December 31, 2002	$150,000

prepared on the last day that the Income Statement covers, so if the Income Statement is for the period ending December 31, 2002, the Balance Sheet would be as on December 31, 2002. You can state the date in a variety of formats. All of the following are acceptable:

As on December 31, 2002

December 31, 2002

On December 31, 2002

The following are typical accounts that are classified as assets, liabilities, and equity accounts. (These accounts are defined later on in the book. There is no reason why you need to know the definitions at this point, but if you are curious, you can turn to the glossary.)

Assets	Liabilities	Equity
Cash	Accounts payable	Common stock
Accounts receivable	Salaries payable	Paid-in capital
Prepaid expenses	Taxes payable	Retained earnings
Inventory	Unearned revenue	
Land	Notes payable	
Building	Bonds payable	
Equipment	Mortgage payable	
Vehicles		

A good general rule of thumb is that any account that has the word *receivable* in its title will be an asset, and any account that has the word *payable* in its title will be a liability. Any account that has the word *expense* in its title is likely to be classified as an expense on the Income Statement, except for

the account Prepaid expenses, which is an asset. Any account
with the word *income* or *revenue* in its title is classified as revenue on the Income Statement, except for the account Unearned revenue, which is a liability.

A sample Balance Sheet is shown in Figure 2-3.

On the Balance Sheet, the largest numbers in each section
are not necessarily listed first. On the asset side of the Balance
Sheet, the accounts are listed in order of their liquidity. Liquidity means nearness to cash. Cash is listed first, since cash is
already cash. Each current asset is then listed in the order in
which it is expected to become cash. Accounts receivable

FIGURE 2-3

Jeffry Haber Company
Balance Sheet
December 31, 2002

Assets:	
Cash	$ 75,000
Accounts receivable	25,000
Inventory	200,000
Prepaid expenses	50,000
Total Assets	$350,000
Liabilities:	
Accounts payable	$50,000
Salaries payable	75,000
Notes payable	65,000
Total Liabilities	$190,000
Stockholders' Equity:	
Common stock	$ 10,000
Retained earnings	150,000
Total Stockholder's Equity	$160,000
Total Liabilities and Stockholder's Equity	$350,000

comes second, since this company believes that its accounts receivable will be collected prior to the other assets being turned into cash.

On the liability side, the accounts are listed in the order in which they are expected to be satisfied (a fancy way of saying paid). The order of the equity accounts is defined by custom and tradition.

There is a special type of Balance Sheet called a classified Balance Sheet. In a classified Balance Sheet, the assets are separated into current and noncurrent (or long-term; the names *noncurrent* and *long-term* are synonymous in accounting) assets, and the liabilities are similarly classified as current and noncurrent. Included in the current section of the assets are those assets that are expected to be turned into cash or used up within the next year. Assets that are not expected to be turned into cash or used up within the next year are classified as noncurrent. Current liabilities are those liabilities that are expected to be paid during the next year. Noncurrent liabilities are those liabilities that are expected to be paid sometime after next year.

We have talked about three of the statements (the Income Statement, the Statement of Retained Earnings, and the Balance Sheet). Which statement do you prepare first? This is strictly a matter of preference; however, as a general rule, it makes the most sense to prepare the Income Statement first, then the Statement of Retained Earnings, and then the Balance Sheet. (The Statement of Cash Flows will be dealt with in a later chapter and is not discussed here.)

Why does that order make sense? To complete the Balance Sheet, the ending amount of Retained earnings is needed. This number comes from the Statement of Retained Earnings, so it makes sense to prepare the Statement of Retained Earnings prior to preparing the Balance Sheet. In order to complete the Statement of Retained Earnings, the amount of net income is required, and this comes from the Income Statement. Therefore, it makes sense to prepare the Income Statement prior to preparing the Statement of Retained Earnings.

Income Statement

Net Income

Statement of Retained Earnings

Ending Balance of Retained Earnings

Balance Sheet

Thus, while the statements may be prepared in any order, if you prepare them in a different sequence, you will not be able to finish the statement you are working on without stopping and going to work on another statement. Eventually they will all be completed, but it will involve some jumping around.

Summary

This chapter covered the end result of financial accounting, the preparation of financial statements. Now we jump back to the beginning of the accounting process and look at how the information gets recorded in order to be available to be put on the financial statements.

3

The Accounting Process

We started with the end product of the accounting process, the financial statements. The steps involved in getting to the financial statements are:

- Journalize
- Post
- Trial balance
- Adjustments
- Financial statements
- Close

These steps include some words we haven't used before. They will be explained later in the chapter.

Journalize

Journalizing is the process of taking transactions and turning them into a form (a journal entry) that can be captured by the financial accounting system. Not everything that happens in the course of a business day requires that a journal entry be made. If you get a letter from a customer praising your product, no journal entry is required. If a customer calls and asks your hours of operation, no journal entry is required. A journal entry is required only when there is a change in an account balance.

With the journal entry, we get into debits and credits. Debits and credits are the left-hand and right-hand sides of a journal entry. They are also a standard shorthand way of saying whether we are increasing or decreasing the balance in an account. In making a journal entry, it is standard practice to list the account(s) getting the debit first and the account(s) getting the credit second. It is also standard to offset the credit entry a little to the right. In addition, it is common to give the date of the transaction and a short description explaining why the entry is being made. A standard journal entry in which we are increasing (debiting) Cash and increasing (crediting) Sales would be:

```
XX/XX/XX        Cash         10,000
                Sales               10,000
                To record cash sales
```

(Whenever you see the notation "XX/XX/XX," it means that a date would typically be included.)

The sample journal entry provides a debit to Cash (which will increase the balance of the Cash account) and a credit to

Sales (which will increase the balance of the Sales account). How do we know when debits will increase or decrease an account? We know the effect debits and credits have from the accounting equation.

The Accounting Equation

The accounting equation is the algebraic formula:

$$Assets = Liabilities + Equity$$

You may recognize the terms *assets, liabilities,* and *equity* from the Balance Sheet. Remember that on the Balance Sheet, the asset section total was equal to the sum of the liability and equity section totals. This is the accounting equation.

From the Balance Sheet, we know that the components of equity are Common stock and Retained earnings. Thus, we can replace equity in the accounting equation with Common stock and Retained earnings:

$$Assets = Liabilities + Common\ stock + Retained\ earnings$$

From the Statement of Retained Earnings, we know that ending Retained earnings are equal to beginning Retained earnings plus net income minus dividends. We can therefore replace Retained earnings with these accounts in the equation:

$$Assets = Liabilities + Common\ stock + Beginning\ retained\ earnings + Net\ income - Dividends$$

From the Income Statement, we know that net income is equal to revenues minus expenses. Thus, we can replace net income in the equation with revenues minus expenses. After doing this, the equation becomes:

Assets = Liabilities + Common stock + Beginning retained earnings + Revenues − Expenses − Dividends

Since this is an algebraic equation, we can take the items that are subtracted and move them from the right side of the equation to the left side:

Assets + Expenses + Dividends = Liabilities + Common stock + Beginning retained earnings + Revenues

The reason we went through these steps to get the accounting equation in this form is to be able to explain the effect of debits and credits on the various accounts (see Figure 3-1). For the accounts to the left of the equal sign (assets, expenses, and dividends), debits will increase the balance and credits will decrease the balance. For the accounts to the right of the equal sign (liabilities, common stock, beginning retained earnings, and revenues), debits will decrease the balance and credits will increase the balance.

FIGURE 3-1			
Assets, Expenses, Dividends		**Liabilities, Common Stock, Beginning Retained Earnings, Revenues**	
+	−	−	+

Post

When we post, we take the journal entry and transfer the amount of the debit to the associated account in the general ledger, and we do the same for the credit. The general ledger is a book in which each account has its own page. Each page is considered a "T" account, so named because in the old days a large "T" was drawn on the page. The name of the account was written across the top. The left side was used for the debits, and the right side was used for the credits (consistent with our previous statement that debits are on the left and credits on the right). In our sample entry, we were debiting $10,000 to the Cash account and crediting $10,000 to the Sales account. The T account for the Cash account is shown in Figure 3-2, and the T account for the Sales account is shown in Figure 3-3.

Any time you want to figure out the balance in an account, you take all the debits and add them to get the total debits. Then you take all the credits and add them to get the total credits. Then you subtract the total debits from the total credits or vice versa and write the difference on whichever side is larger. For example, if the Cash account had debits of $10,000, $20,000, and $5,000 and there was one credit of $15,000, the account would have a debit balance of $20,000. [The total debits are $10,000 + $20,000 + $5,000 = $35,000, and the

FIGURE 3-2

Cash

10,000	

FIGURE 3-3
Sales

	10,000

total credits are $15,000. Subtracting the total debits and total credits produces $20,000 ($35,000 − $15,000), which we write on the larger side, in this case the debit side.] The T account for this situation is shown in Figure 3-4.

Another way to show the balance in the T account is by writing the subtotals for debits and credits and then writing the balance underneath the larger side, as shown in Figure 3-5.

It is customary to draw a line before writing the balance. Today, general ledger pages often do not have a large T drawn on them, but the essential information remains the same—the name of the account, debits in a column on the left, and credits in a column on the right. There can be additional columns

FIGURE 3-4
Cash

10,000	15,000
20,000	
5,000	
20,000	

FIGURE 3-5	
Cash	
10,000	15,000
20,000	
5,000	
35,000	15,000
20,000	

for a running balance (see Figure 3-6), or the balance can be written under the larger side. The basics of the T account are applicable to any general ledger page in any manual or computerized system.

Trial Balance

The trial balance is a listing of all the accounts and their balances. Usually, there are two columns on the trial balance, one for debits and one for credits. You prepare the trial balance by going through the general ledger, taking the balance from each

FIGURE 3-6			
Cash			
Date	Debit	Credit	Balance
7/01/01	10,000		10,000
7/02/01	20,000		30,000
7/14/01		15,000	15,000
7/15/01	5,000		20,000

page (with each page being a different account), and listing those balances. When you are finished, you total the debits column and then total the credits column, and hopefully they will be equal. An example of a trial balance is given in Figure 3-7.

The trial balance does two things. First, it shows that total debits equal total credits. It is not possible to prepare a set of financial statements that are correct if you do not start with a trial balance that balances. One reason the trial balance may not balance is that you forgot to list an account. You might have also listed a balance in the wrong column or entered the wrong amount. What do you do if the debits do not equal the credits? Since the trial balance is a listing of every account and its balance, it offers lots of opportunity for a mistake in writing down a number.

Finding Errors

Let's assume that the total debits do not equal the total credits. We will use the trial balance in Figure 3-7 to illustrate the techniques in finding errors. The first step is to find the difference. Let's say our mistake was to list the Notes payable as 56,000 instead of 65,000. Therefore, the balance in the debit column would still be 550,500; however, the credits would total 541,500. The difference between the two columns is 9,000 (550,500 − 541,500). The second step is to take the difference and divide it by 9. If the result is an integer (no remainder), the error could be a transposition error. A transposition error occurs when you flip two adjacent numbers. Our difference is 9,000, so when we divide by 9, we get 1,000. Since the difference divides evenly by 9, we may have a transposition error.

The number we get after we divide by 9 provides a lot of

FIGURE 3-7		
Jeffry Haber Company **Trial Balance** **For the Year Ended December 31, 2002**		
	Debits	**Credits**
Sales		250,000
Interest income		500
Payroll	125,000	
Payroll taxes	20,000	
Rent	10,000	
Telephone	7,000	
Office supplies	3,000	
Cash	75,000	
Accounts receivable	25,000	
Inventory	200,000	
Prepaid expenses	50,000	
Accounts payable		50,000
Salaries payable		75,000
Notes payable		65,000
Common stock		10,000
Retained earnings		100,000
Dividends	35,500	
Total	550,500	550,500

information about the potential error we are looking for. Since our number after dividing was 1,000, if the error is a transposition, we are looking for a transposition in which the numbers that were flipped are consecutive (for example, flipping 1 and 2, 2 and 3, 3 and 4, and so on). That is the information contained in the first digit. If the first digit of the number we got after dividing was 2, then we would be looking for a transposition involving numbers that were two places away (for example, 1 and 3, 2 and 4, 3 and 5, and so on).

The number of zeros provides information about which digits were transposed (if this is a transposition error). Since the number we got after dividing was 1,000, we would look in the thousands and ten-thousands places for the transposition. Armed with this information, we are looking for a number on our trial balance in which there are consecutive numbers listed in the thousands and ten-thousands places. The only number that meets these criteria is the amount for Notes payable—56,000. Going back to the general ledger, we see that we wrote the figure incorrectly.

Another type of error involves writing the amount in the wrong column. Suppose we entered the Interest income in the debit column instead of the credit column. The total of the debit column would be 551,000, and the total of the credit column would be 550,000. Again, the first step is to find the difference. In this case, the difference is 1,000 ($551,000—$550,000). When we divide the difference by 9, we find that it does not divide evenly, so we are not looking for a transposition error. The next error to look for is entering the amount in the wrong column. If we take the difference and divide it by 2, we get 500 (1,000/2). Now we scan the trial balance looking for an amount of 500. The only account that meets this criterion is Interest income. We check the general ledger and find that the amount should be in the credit column, but we mistakenly put it in the debit column. Problem solved.

Another type of error that may occur is leaving a number off the trial balance entirely. If this happens, we will look for the first two errors, since they are more common, but we will not find the mistake. The third thing to do is to take our difference and look through the general ledger for an account with a balance of that amount.

Let's say we left Accounts payable off the trial balance. The total of the debit column would be 550,500, and the total of the credit column would be 500,500. The difference is 50,000 (550,500 − 500,500). Going through our steps, we first divide the difference by 9. The difference does not divide evenly by 9, so this is not a transposition error. We then take the difference and divide it in half, giving a result of 25,000. There is no amount of 25,000 in the trial balance, so we did not enter an amount in the wrong column. We then go back to the general ledger and look for an account with a balance of 50,000. We see that Accounts payable has a balance of 50,000, so we look to see if we listed it on the trial balance. It is not listed, so we have found our error.

The second thing the trial balance does is to make it easy to prepare the financial statements. We have a listing of all the accounts and their balances on one page, and this is a convenient list to use to prepare the statements. The order of the accounts on the trial balance should be the same as the order in which they are listed in the general ledger. Some accountants like to list the revenue and expense accounts first, since they will prepare the Income Statement first, and this lets them start at the top of the trial balance and work their way through the financial statements.

Rest of the Process

Adjusting entries and closing entries will be covered in Chapter
18. The next step in learning financial accounting is to learn
the actual recording of transactions. We get information into
the general ledger by journalizing transactions (making journal
entries) and then posting them to the general ledger. If the
information is not in the general ledger, it won't be on the
financial statements, so this is a critical step. The financial
statements will be only as good as the information they contain.

Summary

This chapter described the accounting process and discussed
each step from the point at which a journal entry is made
through the trial balance. The chapter also explained the accounting equation and expanded the equation to provide a
framework for understanding when debits and credits increase
or decrease the various accounts.

The next chapter will specifically look at how to make journal entries when transactions occur that need to be captured
in the accounting records.

CHAPTER 4

Making the Entries

For the beginning student, the hardest aspect of accounting to learn is often whether each account is classified as an asset, a liability, an equity account, revenue, or expense, and when to debit or credit each account. This chapter is designed to provide a reference point in helping to understand how the entries are made. Learning where the accounts are classified is largely a matter of memorization. The Balance Sheet contains the assets, liabilities, and equity accounts (think BALE—*B*alance sheet: *A*ssets, *L*iabilities, and *E*quity). The Income Statement contains the revenues and expenses (think IRE—*I*ncome statement: *R*evenues and *E*xpenses). Every account can be classified as an asset, liability, equity account, revenue, or expense.

As a general rule, assets are things that you own, such as cash, inventory, investments, land, buildings, and equipment, and things that are owed to you, such as accounts receivable and notes receivable. Liabilities are things that you owe, such as accounts payable, salaries payable, interest payable, and notes payable. As stated in Chapter 2, a basic guide is that any account with the word *receivable* in its title is an asset, and any account with the word *payable* in its title is a liability.

Revenues are the money earned by the company, such as sales or interest income. Except for the account Unearned revenue (which is a liability), any time you see the word *revenue* in the account name, you should figure that it is a part of the revenues section of the Income Statement. Except for the account Prepaid expenses (which is an asset), any time you see the word *expense* in an account title, you should figure that the account goes on the Income Statement in the expenses section.

Analogies to Personal Life

Think of your personal life. You go to work, and you get paid. Let's say your salary was $1,000 for the week. When you get paid, you get a check for $1,000 (let's forget about taxes to make the example simple). Journal entries always contain at least one debit and one credit, and the total of the debits equals the total of the credits. So what needs to be recorded? You now have $1,000, so that has to be recorded—we have to increase the balance in the Cash account (also called the checking account). We increase Cash by debiting it, so that is the first part of the journal entry: a debit to Cash.

We can't stop there, because now we need a credit in order to balance the entry. Let's think about this. We got $1,000 because we worked for it. We have recorded the money we now have; what remains is to record that we earned the money—to record the revenue. To increase Revenue, we credit it, which works out perfectly, since we need a credit to balance the journal entry.

If we pay $300 for rent, we need to record that we no longer have that $300 in our checking account, so we need to reduce the account balance. We do this by crediting Cash. Now we need a debit. Since we made a payment for rent, we need to record the expense. We do this by debiting Rent expense, and our entry balances.

Some accounts tend to be debited and credited together. A business that does a lot of sales for cash will often debit Cash and credit Revenue (or it might call the account Sales instead of Revenue). A company that does a lot of business on credit will tend to debit Accounts receivable and credit Sales when the sale is made (increasing the Accounts receivable account to record that the company is now owed money, and also recording the increase in the Sales account). The company will also tend to debit Cash and credit Accounts receivable when payments are received (to increase the Cash balance, since the customer has paid, and to reduce the Accounts receivable balance, since it is no longer owed the money).

When bills are received, the company records what the bill is for (utility expense, rent expense, repair expense, and so on) by debiting the appropriate expense account. It also records that it owes money by crediting Accounts payable. When the company pays the bill, it records a debit to Accounts payable (to reduce the balance in Accounts payable, since it no longer owes the money) and a credit to Cash (to show that the balance in its checking account has decreased).

Some Examples

A couple of examples may make things clearer. What follows is a list of transactions, followed by the entries that would be made.

On January 3, 2002, the company receives $1,000 for services rendered:

1/03/02	Cash	1,000	
	Revenue		1,000
	To record payment for services		

On January 25, 2002, the company pays rent of $200:

1/25/02	Rent expense	200	
	Cash		200
	To record rent expense		

On February 18, 2002, the company provides services and bills the customer $1,200:

2/18/02	Accounts receivable	1,200	
	Revenue		1,200
	To record services rendered and billed		

On April 7, 2002, the company pays salaries of $2,000:

4/07/02	Salary expense	2,000	
	Cash		2,000
	To record salary expense		

On May 4, 2002, the company receives the money that it is owed for the services provided:

5/04/02	Cash	1,200	
	Accounts receivable		1,200
	To record payment on account		

On June 28, 2002, the company receives a bill for repairs done to some equipment in the amount of $850:

6/28/02	Repair expense	850
	Accounts payable	850
	To record bill for repairs	

On July 1, 2002, the company is prepaid $1,000 for services to be provided:

7/01/02	Cash	1,000
	Unearned revenue	1,000
	To record prepaid services	

On July 14, 2002, the company provides $500 of the services that were prepaid on July 1:

7/14/02	Unearned revenue	500
	Revenue	500
	To record services provided	

Summary

This chapter took specific instances of transactions that occur frequently in business and translated these transactions into journal entries. A thought process that can be applied to any situation that may occur is also provided.

The next chapters will expand the discussion of the various accounts and review all the elements of the financial statements in more detail.

CHAPTER 5

Assets

Assets can be thought of as the things you own, the things you have rights to, and expenses that have been paid for and have not yet been used up. The things a company owns include cash, investments, inventory, land, buildings, equipment, vehicles, furniture, and fixtures. Assets that represent items the company has rights to include licenses, trademarks, copyrights, and franchises. An asset that represents an expense that has been paid for and not yet used up is a prepaid expense.

Assets are often divided into current and noncurrent (sometimes called long-term). Current assets are those assets that are expected to be turned into cash or used up within the next twelve months. Typical current assets are Cash, Accounts receivable, Inventory, Marketable securities, and Prepaid expenses.

Noncurrent assets are those assets that are not going to be turned into cash or used up within the next twelve months.

Noncurrent assets are further broken into the following categories:

- Fixed assets (also called Plant, Property, and Equipment):

  Land

  Land improvements

  Leasehold improvements

  Buildings

  Equipment

  Vehicles

  Machinery

  Furniture

  Fixtures

- Intangible assets:

  Patents

  Copyrights

  Trademarks

  Franchises

- Investments

- Other assets

The different types of assets will be discussed individually in the following chapters.

CHAPTER 6

Cash

Cash is the most coveted of all assets. It can be converted into any other asset, and therefore is viewed as the most desirable. A company can stay in business without making a profit (for example, Amazon.com raised enough capital to last it through many years of not making a profit), but it cannot stay in business without cash (think of all the failed dot-com companies).

Petty Cash

Cash includes currency and coins, although most businesses do not keep much of this type of cash around. Also included as a part of cash are the balances kept at banking and financial institutions. These balances include savings and checking accounts. The cash a business keeps on hand is called *petty cash*. If you order a pizza for the staff to eat at lunch, the delivery person is not going to want to prepare a bill and then wait two weeks for a check. The delivery person will want payment at the time of delivery, so businesses usually keep some cash handy for these minor payments. A petty cash box handles the chore nicely.

Let's say the company decides that $200 is the right amount of cash to have on hand. On February 19, 2002, it prepares a check to be cashed (or someone visits the ATM if the firm has a card) and gets $200 from the company checking account. Now the petty cash box has $200 cash in it. The entry to record this is:

2/19/02	Petty cash	200
	Cash	200
	To set up the Petty cash account	

Remember, debits increase assets and credits decrease assets (both Petty cash and the checking account are current assets), so what the entry has done is increase the balance in Petty cash (it is now $200) and decrease the balance in the checking account (by $200).

When the pizza arrives, the bill is $10 plus a $2 tip. So now the petty cash box has $188 in cash ($200 − $12) and a receipt for $12, for a total of $200. If everything is done right, the sum of the cash in the box plus the receipts will always total $200. At some point there will be only a small amount of cash in the box (and a lot of receipts). On April 7, 2002, the person responsible gathers the receipts and sends them to the accounting department so that a check can be prepared. Let's continue the example and send the only receipt in the box to the accounting department to replenish petty cash.

The check to be made out will equal the total of the receipts, in this case $12. In every journal entry, there is usually one part of the entry that is easy to figure out. Since a check for $12 will be coming out of the checking account, it is easy to get the credit part of the entry—a credit of $12 to the checking account (or Cash account). The debit is a little trickier. Most beginning accounting students would immediately say that the debit should go to Petty cash, since the $12 check is going to be used to replenish the balance. However logical this may seem, it is incorrect. Once we make the initial entry to Petty cash, we will never debit or credit this account again unless we are changing the permanent balance in the account. Right now the general ledger shows the balance in Petty cash as $200, which is exactly right. If we were to debit the $12 to Petty cash, the general ledger would show a balance of $212, which is wrong. Whenever we replenish petty cash, the debit goes to whatever the expenses were for. In this case, the expense was for pizza for an office lunch. Therefore, the debit goes to Meals and entertainment, Office expense, or whichever expense account the company would usually put this type of expenditure in. The entry is:

```
4/07/02   Meals and entertainment      12
               Cash                          12
          To replenish petty cash
```

Bank Reconciliation

The company keeps track of its checking account balance, and each month it receives a statement from the bank. The company needs to make sure that it has recorded everything properly, and it is a good idea to make sure that the bank has recorded everything properly as well (ask your friends—it will be hard to find someone who hasn't been the victim of a bank error). The mechanism for checking the general ledger balance (the "book balance") against the bank statement balance (the "bank balance") is the *bank reconciliation.*

It is unusual for the book balance to match the bank balance. For example, if you mailed a check on the last day of the month, you would have reduced your checking account balance, but the check would not have made it to your bank yet, and therefore it would not have been subtracted from the bank balance on the bank statement just received. This is an example of an *outstanding check,* which is a check that the company has written and subtracted from its balance but that has not yet been recorded by the bank. If you take a deposit to the bank on the last day of the month, it is possible that the bank will not show it as a deposit until the first day of the next month. However, the company will include the deposit as part of its checking account balance on the last day of the month. This is an example of a *deposit in transit,* which is a deposit that the company includes as part of its cash balance but that the bank has not yet included.

There may also be items that are part of the bank balance that have not yet been recorded in the company's checking account. Common examples of this are service charges, bank fees, interest added to the account, and wire transfers (deposits), which are common among companies that accept credit and debit cards.

There are three ways to prepare the bank reconciliation:

1. Take the book balance and reconcile it to the bank balance.

2. Take the bank balance and reconcile it to the book balance.

3. Take the book balance and reconcile it to an adjusted cash balance, then take the bank balance and reconcile

it to the adjusted cash balance (the word *reconcile* means making adjustments to arrive at another number).

I prefer the third method, taking both the book and bank balances and reconciling them to an adjusted cash balance. When this method is used, any reconciling items needed to get the book balance to the adjusted cash balance will require the preparation of journal entries to adjust the book balance. Any reconciling items needed to get the bank balance to the adjusted cash balance will not require journal entries.

When the bank statement arrives, the first step is to note which checks were returned with the statement (have cleared the bank or, in other words, were recorded by the bank). A sample bank statement is presented in Figure 6-1.

Most companies go through their cash disbursements (a listing of all checks sent, usually incorporating columns that detail the payee, the date, the amount, and the check number) and put a mark next to the checks that have come back with the bank statement. Any check without a mark will be put on a list of outstanding checks. The company will do the same thing with deposits: Any deposit that does not have a mark indicating that it appears on the bank statement will be put on a list of deposits in transit. The company then goes through the bank statement and notes any increases or decreases that the bank has made to the account (aside from the items we already know about, such as the checks we wrote or the deposits we made). Any of these items that have not been put into the general ledger will be part of the adjustments necessary to get the book balance to the adjusted balance. The general ledger checking account is presented in Figure 6-2. (The check number is not usually put in the general ledger, but by doing so we can use the general ledger account as a substitute for the cash disbursement list.)

FIGURE 6-1

FIRST BANK OF AMERICA
1234 Main Street
Anytown, US 12345

Jeffry Haber Company	For the period 12/1/02–12/31/02	
5678 Main Street	Starting Balance	$6,250.50
Anytown, US 12345	Deposits and other credits	$1,000.00
	Checks and other debits	$4,724.75
Account Number 3322118	Closing Balance	$2,525.75

	Debits	Credits	Balance
12/1/2002 Opening balance			$6,250.50
12/2/2002 Deposit		$1,000.00	$7,250.50
12/7/2002 Deposited item returned	$500.00		$6,750.50
12/7/2002 Service charge on returned item	$25.00		$6,725.50
12/8/2002 Cleared check #1117	$350.00		$6,375.50
12/15/2002 Cleared check #1118	$1,250.00		$5,125.50
12/22/2002 Cleared check #1119	$2,599.75		$2,525.75
12/31/2002 Closing balance			$2,525.75

Let's assume that the following checks have not cleared the bank:

Check #	Amount
1120	$ 800.00
1121	125.00
1122	50.50
1123	35.25
Total	$1,010.75

The only deposit that has not cleared the bank was in the amount of $2,500.00. In addition, the bank statement shows

FIGURE 6-2

Checking

6,250.50	
1,000.00	350.00 #1117
2,500.00	1,250.00 #1118
	2,599.75 #1119
	800.00 #1120
	125.00 #1121
	50.50 #1122
	35.25 #1123
4,540.00	

that a deposit in the amount of $500.00 that the company made was returned and that a fee in the amount of $25.00 was assessed. The check for $500.00 was originally a payment on account. After going through the general ledger balance and the bank statement, the items that have not been crossed off (see Figure 6-3) are used for the reconciliation.

The reconciliation is prepared as follows:

	Book	Bank
Starting balance	$4,540.00	$2,525.75
Add: Deposits in transit		2,500.00
Subtotal	4,540.00	5,025.75
Less: Outstanding checks		1,010.75
Less: Returned check	500.00	
Less: Bank fee	25.00	
Adjusted cash balance	$4,015.00	$4,015.00

The reconciliation is complete when the adjusted cash balances are equal. Any adjustment on the book side requires the

FIGURE 6-3

FIRST BANK OF AMERICA
1234 Main Street
Anytown, US 12345

Jeffry Haber Company   **For the period 12/1/02–12/31/02**

5678 Main Street

Anytown, US 12345

Account Number 3322118

Starting Balance		$6,250.50
Deposits and other credits		$1,000.00
Checks and other debits		$4,724.75
Closing Balance		$2,525.75

	Debits	Credits	Balance
12/1/2002 Opening balance			$6,250.50
12/2/2002 Deposit		$1,000.00	$7,250.50
12/7/2002 Deposited item returned	$500.00		$6,750.50
12/7/2002 Service charge on returned item	$25.00		$6,725.50
12/8/2002 Cleared check #1117	$350.00		$6,375.50
12/15/2002 Cleared check #1118	$1,250.00		$5,125.50
12/22/2002 Cleared check #1119	$2,599.75		$2,525.75
12/31/2002 Closing balance			$2,525.75

Checking

beg bal	6,250.50	
12/01/02	1,000.00	350.00
12/31/02	2,500.00	1,250.00
		2,599.75
		800.00
		125.00
		50.50
		35.25
	4,540.00	

preparation of a journal entry. The starting balance for the book column was taken from the general ledger; the starting balance for the bank column was taken from the bank statement. There are two entries to be made.

An entry must be made to record the return of the deposit of $500.00, which was a payment on account. The original entry made on November 25, 2002, when the check for $500 was received, was:

11/25/02	Cash	500	
	Accounts receivable		500
	To record payment on account		

This recorded an increase in the checking account balance and a reduction in the customer's accounts receivable balance. Since the payment was returned, the customer still owes that amount. We have to add the $500 back to the customer's receivable balance, and we also have to reduce the checking account balance. The entry is therefore:

12/07/02	Accounts receivable	500	
	Cash		500
	To record returned check		

An entry must also be made for the bank fee, which requires a reduction of the checking account balance (credit) and a debit to record the expense. The account in which the expense is recorded can be titled Bank service charges, Office expense, or something similar.

12/07/02	Bank service charges	25	
	Cash		25
	To record service charge on returned check		

7

Accounts Receivable

Accounts receivable are amounts owed to the company by its customers and clients for services or goods provided. Accounts receivable arise from sales transactions. Sometimes a company will sell to an individual on credit, but more often transactions involving credit are business-to-business transactions. As individuals going about our daily lives, we are accustomed to paying for things when we buy them. As an example of a situation (to which many people can relate) in which a person might owe a business money, think of a doctor's office. Generally, doctors prefer to be paid at the time the services are rendered. However, sometimes we forget to bring a check with us to the office (I know this has happened to me on occasion). When this happens, the office will either give us a bill or mail us one. In the doctor's accounting records, the doctor will want to record that he or she provided service and earned revenue (by crediting Revenue), and also to record that the patient owes the doctor money (by debiting Accounts receiv-

41

able). In our accounting records, we will want to record that
we owe the doctor money (by crediting Accounts payable) and
that we incurred medical expense (by debiting whatever expense account this type of item would be charged to). In the
business-to-business world, when you make a sale to a customer
and the customer is billed, the entry to record the sale is:

```
XX/XX/XX   Accounts receivable      1,500
               Sales                          1,500
           To record sale on account
```

When payment is received, the entry is:

```
XX/XX/XX   Cash                     1,500
               Accounts receivable     1,500
           To record payment on account
```

If the payment is for less than the full amount owed, then
you simply record the amount of the actual payment rather
than the full amount owed. The difference between the full
amount and the amount owed is the amount still owed by the
customer. Let's say that the customer paid $1,200 instead of
the full balance. The entry to record the receipt of the $1,200
would be:

```
XX/XX/XX   Cash                     1,200
               Accounts receivable    1,200
           To record payment on account
```

Control Account/Subsidiary Ledger

If business is going well, you can imagine that a company
could have a lot of customers, and therefore a lot of accounts

receivable. If it were your company, you would want to keep track of what each customer owed you so that you could make sure that your customers were paying promptly. The general ledger is not the place for details about accounts; it should be used to summarize the company's financial information. To be more efficient, we use what's called a *control account* in the general ledger, and we also use a subsidiary ledger in which the details of each customer's account are kept. The total of the subsidiary ledger will equal the control account (the balance in the general ledger). The subsidiary ledger is set up like the general ledger. There will be one page for each customer that details the amounts that the customer owes, the amounts the customer has paid, and the difference between the two (the balance still owed). Figure 7-1 is an example of the subsidiary accounts and the general ledger control account for a company that has three customers. (Three has been chosen for simplicity; usually a company would have substantially more customers than that.)

At the end of the month, ABC Company owes $2,000, DEF Company owes $5,500, and GHI Company owes $2,400, for a total of $9,900. This is the balance shown in the general ledger control account. The total of all the bills sent is the debit to the control account ($8,000 + $10,500 + $16,900 = $35,400), and the credit is the total of all the payments made ($6,000 + $5,000 + $14,500 = $25,500). Figure 7-2 shows what the general ledger account would look like if we included all the detail and did not utilize a subsidiary account.

Even in this simple example of only three companies for a very brief period of time, it would be tedious and time-consuming to figure out what each company owes using the general ledger. Now consider that there will be many months (or

FIGURE 7-1

General ledger control account:

Accounts receivable

35,400.00	25,500.00
9,900.00	

Subsidiary ledger accounts:

ABC Company

Charges	Payments	Balance
1,000.00	500.00	500.00
2,000.00	500.00	2,000.00
3,000.00	1,000.00	4,000.00
2,000.00	4,000.00	2,000.00
8,000.00	6,000.00	2,000.00

DEF Company

Charges	Payments	Balance
2,000.00	2,000.00	0.00
2,000.00	2,000.00	0.00
2,000.00	1,000.00	1,000.00
1,500.00		2,500.00
3,000.00		5,500.00
10,500.00	5,000.00	5,500.00

GHI Company

Charges	Payments	Balance
4,500.00	4,500.00	0.00
6,500.00	5,000.00	1,500.00
3,500.00	5,000.00	0.00
2,400.00		2,400.00
16,900.00	14,500.00	2,400.00

FIGURE 7-2		
Accounts receivable		
ABC	1,000.00	500.00 ABC
DEF	2,000.00	2,000.00 DEF
GHI	4,500.00	4,500.00 GHI
ABC	2,000.00	500.00 ABC
DEF	2,000.00	2,000.00 DEF
GHI	6,500.00	5,000.00 GHI
ABC	3,000.00	1,000.00 ABC
DEF	2,000.00	1,000.00 DEF
GHI	3,500.00	5,000.00 GHI
ABC	2,000.00	4,000.00 ABC
DEF	1,500.00	
GHI	2,400.00	
DEF	3,000.00	
	9,900.00	

years) of activity and many customers. The subsidiary ledger/
control account system is the easiest way to track receivables.

Bad Debts

What happens if a customer isn't going to pay? Suppose the
customer goes bankrupt, or the account is three years old.
There is no sense maintaining the balance, sending statements, and perhaps following up with telephone calls. Sooner
or later the company has to realize that it is not going to get
paid and remove the amount from Accounts receivable. There
are two methods that can be used: the direct write-off method
and the allowance method.

Direct Write-Off Method

The direct write-off method removes (writes off) a balance
from the Accounts receivable account when the company de-

termines that the likelihood of receiving payment has diminished to negligible proportions. With this method, when the company writes off an account, it can attach a customer's name to the amount being written off, and the subsidiary ledger can be adjusted. The entry using the direct write-off method to write off an accounts receivable is:

```
XX/XX/XX    Bad debt expense                    2,000
               Accounts receivable—ABC          2,000
            To write off receivable balance
```

A shortcoming of this method is that by the time you realize that you are not going to get paid, a long period has gone by. One of the key elements of good financial reporting is the *matching principle.* The matching principle requires that we attempt to match expenses with the revenues they relate to. In the case of writing off bad debts, the matching principle says that we should write off the receivable in the same year in which we received the revenue that relates to it. Therefore, one of the rules of accounting states that the direct write-off method is usually not acceptable. The preferred method is the allowance method.

Allowance Method

The allowance method recognizes that timing the write-off so that it coincides with the period in which the revenue was generated means that we cannot be sure which specific accounts will go bad (become uncollectible). Despite this, the company has some experience with customers' payment practices. Perhaps it can equate future bad debts to a percentage of sales. For example, based on experience, the company may be able to say that 1 percent of credit sales will eventually go bad. If net credit sales for the year were $5,000,000 (notice that we do not include cash sales), then the amount to set up as the allowance is $50,000 (1 percent times $5,000,000). The entry to record the allowance is:

XX/XX/XX	Bad debt expense	50,000	
	Allowance for doubtful accounts		50,000
	To record bad debt expense for the year		

The account called Allowance for doubtful accounts is a current asset. Remember what we said before: Assets are increased by debits and decreased by credits. In this case, however, we have an asset account that is increased by a credit. This type of account is known as a "contra" account; in this instance, it is a contra-asset account. The Allowance account will be used to adjust the balance of the Accounts receivable account. On the Balance Sheet, the allowance account will come right after Accounts receivable and be a reduction of it. Here are two examples of how the accounts receivable and the allowance might be shown on the Balance Sheet:

Alternative 1:	Accounts receivable	$1,200,000
	Less: Allowance for doubtful accounts	50,000
	Net accounts receivable	$1,150,000
Alternative 2:	Accounts receivable (net of allowance of 50,000)	$1,150,000

Instead of estimating bad debt expense based on sales, a company might use a report called the *aging of accounts receivable*. An accounts receivable aging details how much is owed by each customer and how long the amount has been owed. Typical columns are Current, 31–60 days, 61–90 days, 91–120 days, and 120+ days. The older the debts in a column, the higher the percentage that the company would use to estimate the uncollectible portion. Perhaps it would use 10 percent for amounts over 120 days, 5 percent for amounts 91–120 days, and 1 percent for amounts 61–90 days. Figure 7-3 is an aging for the Jeffry Haber Company and the allowance based on the aging.

Using the aging to estimate the allowance tells us what the balance in the Allowance account should be—in this case, $260. We then adjust the balance in the Allowance account to get it to $260. If we checked the general ledger and saw that the balance was a credit of $100, we would need to credit the account by $160 to get the balance to $260 ($260 − $100; see Example A in Figure 7-4). If the balance in the allowance account were a credit of $400, we would need to debit the account by $140 in order to reduce the balance to $260 ($400 −

FIGURE 7-3						
Jeffry Haber Company **Accounts Receivable Aging** **As of December 31, 2002**						
Customer	Total	Current	31–60	61–90	91–120	120+
ABC Comp	2,000.00	500.00	500.00	500.00	500.00	
DEF Comp	5,500.00			3,000.00	1,000.00	1,500.00
GHI Comp	2,400.00	2,400.00				
Total	9,900.00	2,900.00	500.00	3,500.00	1,500.00	1,500.00
Allowance %				1%	5%	10%
Allowance	260.00			35.00	75.00	150.00

	(A) Allowance		(B) Allowance		(C) Allowance	
Current balance		100		400	300	
Entry needed		160	140			560
Desired balance		260		260		260

FIGURE 7-4

$140; see Example B). If the allowance account had a debit balance of $300, then we would need to credit the account by $560 to get the balance to a credit of $260 ($300 + $260; see Example C). Figure 7-4 shows the general ledger accounts for the three examples.

The journal entries for each example are:

Example A

XX/XX/XX	Bad debt expense	160	
	Allowance		160
	To adjust the balance in the Allowance account		

Example B

XX/XX/XX	Allowance	140	
	Bad debt expense		140
	To adjust the balance in the Allowance account		

Example C

```
XX/XX/XX   Bad debt expense              560
           Allowance                         560
           To adjust the balance in the Allowance
           account
```

The allowance is a total representing the amount that, based either on sales or on an accounts receivable aging, the company believes will not be collected. There is no way to associate the allowance with individual customers' balances. However, at some point the company may decide that a certain customer's account is no longer collectible. When using the allowance method, we would write the account off at that time, but we would write it off to the Allowance rather than to Bad debt expense. The entry to write off a particular account when using the allowance method is:

```
XX/XX/XX   Allowance                     XXX
           Accounts receivable               XXX
           To write off an account receivable
```

We simultaneously remove the account from the allowance and from the subsidiary accounts receivable ledger (and from the control account as well).

What happens if the customer pays after we write the account off? The first step is to reverse the entry we made when we wrote the account off:

```
XX/XX/XX   Accounts receivable           XXX
           Allowance                         XXX
           To reinstate accounts receivable balance
```

Now the situation is just what it would have been if we had never written the account off. We now treat the receipt of the check just as we would any payment on account:

XX/XX/XX	Cash	XXX	
	Accounts receivable		XXX
	To record payment on account		

CHAPTER 8

Inventory

Inventory is the goods that companies sell. Companies that provide services and do not sell goods do not have inventory. For those companies that manufacture goods or purchase them for resale, managing inventory is an important part of operations. Inventory is often a company's largest current asset. If the inventory can be sold, it is a good thing; if the inventory is unwanted, it is a real bad thing. Any parent can remember trying to get his or her child a "hot" toy such as Tickle Me Elmo, Teenage Mutant Ninja Turtle Action figures, or a Mighty Morphin Power Ranger, only to find the stores sold out. A couple of months later, the stores are overstocked and these items are being sold at a huge discount. Matching supply with demand is critical, since demand does not remain forever.

Let's say the store we are talking about is a store that sells office supplies. The inventory is piled up in the storeroom in the back and moved out to the sales floor when it is needed. The inventory is an asset, and the store hopes that it will be sold. When it is sold, it becomes an expense (it is classified as Cost of goods sold). Let's take a simple example. We purchase paper clips to sell. When we receive the paper clips from the manufacturer, we need to record that we now have inventory and that we owe the manufacturer some money. Let's say the paper clips cost $500 for the case and we receive them on February 22, 2002. The entry to record the receipt of the paper clips is:

2/22/02	Inventory	500
	Accounts payable	500
	To record receipt of inventory on credit	

Of course, $500 buys a lot of paper clips. Let's say that we are fortunate and we sell all of them during the month of March. We no longer have the inventory; therefore we need to reduce the asset and move the $500 to the Income Statement. We do this by making the following entry:

3/31/02	Cost of goods sold	500
	Inventory	500
	To record reduction of inventory due to sale	

Of course, most stores are getting shipments all the time, and sometimes price changes happen. If we already have a case of paper clips in the back that we paid $450 for and we get a new shipment that costs $500, how do we decide which paper clips we sold? Did they come from the batch that cost $450 or from the batch that cost $500? If we are careful and we monitor which case the paper clips we sold came from, we can always be sure.

But if the stockperson opens both cases and loads the shelf

with boxes from each, there is no way to tell which paper clips are being sold. This type of situation often arises in business. Think of a gas station. It may fill its tank with gas purchased at different times and at different prices. The gas that actually goes into your car is a combination of all the gas that has been put into the tank. Accounting handles this by having the company choose what is known as an *inventory costing method.* The inventory costing method provides the rules that are used to determine what the cost of the items sold was.

There are four basic systems to choose from:

- Specific identification

- First-in, first-out (FIFO)

- Last-in, first-out (LIFO)

- Weighted average

Specific Identification

Specific identification is the easiest system to understand. It can be used in any industry where the goods involved are a few high-priced items that are distinguishable from one another. A good example is the automobile industry. Each car has a vehicle identification number (VIN), so tracking which car was sold is relatively easy. Even though our paper clips have a bar code, every similar box of paper clips has the same bar code. With the VIN, only one car has that exact number.

When we sell the car, we can match the VIN with our records to determine what we paid for the car. That is the amount that is transferred from Inventory to Cost of goods sold.

First-In, First-Out

There is no requirement that the costing method chosen actually follow the physical flow of the goods. If we sold milk, it is not hard to imagine that we would try to sell the oldest milk (the first milk that came into the store) first. In that instance, the FIFO method would follow the physical flow of the goods. To use FIFO, it is necessary to keep detailed records of the number of units in each receipt of inventory and each sale. To illustrate FIFO, LIFO, and weighted average, we will use the same set of figures:

Jan. 4   Receive 1,000 units at a cost of $35 each
Jan. 5   Receive 1,250 units at a cost of $40 each
Jan. 7   Sell 500 units
Jan. 8   Sell 750 units
Jan. 9   Receive 2,000 units at a cost of $42 each
Jan. 10   Sell 1,000 units

There is nothing difficult about figuring out how much the units that were sold cost, if you keep track and go through each step carefully. We can even check our calculations, since we know that whatever was not sold must still remain in the store, and under FIFO the last units in will be the units that will still remain in inventory. The chronology of what happens to the units is shown in Figure 8-1.

During the period of time this example covers, the company purchased 4,250 units (1,000 + 1,250 + 2,000) at a total cost of $169,000 ($35,000 + $50,000 + $84,000) and sold 2,250 units (500 + 750 + 1,000). There are 2,000 units left in inventory (4,250 − 2,250). The value of the units remaining in inventory will be an asset on the Balance Sheet, and the Cost of

			FIGURE 8-1		
Date	Receive	Price	Total	Sell	Balance
Jan. 4	1,000	35	35,000		1,000
Jan. 5	1,250	40	50,000		2,250
Jan. 7				500	1,750
Jan. 8				750	1,000
Jan. 9	2,000	42	84,000		3,000
Jan. 10				1,000	2,000
Total	4,250		169,000	2,250	2,000

goods sold will be an expense on the Income Statement. The inventory costing assumption allows us to assign a cost to the units that were sold and also to value the units left in inventory. The amount we take from Inventory and charge to Cost of goods sold plus the balance left in Inventory must equal $169,000, the total value of the units purchased for resale. The inventory costing assumption allows us to split the $169,000 (which includes inventory purchased at different times at various prices) between the Inventory account (a Balance Sheet item representing what's left) and the Cost of goods sold account (an Income Statement item representing what was sold).

The first sale took place on January 7. FIFO assumes that the units sold came from the earliest units received by the company. In this example, that would be from the lot of 1,000 units that cost $35 each. Therefore, the 500 units sold on January 7 are assumed to have cost $35 each. Our entry is:

```
1/07/02     Cost of goods sold        17,500
                Inventory                    17,500
            To record the sale of 500 units that cost $35
```

Please note that we are only concerned with making the entries to transfer the cost of goods sold. There would also be an entry to record the sale, which would involve a debit to Cash and a credit to Sales. This is discussed in Chapter 17.

The next sale takes place on January 8, when we sell 750 units. We still have 500 units left from the first lot of 1,000 units (after deducting the 500 that we sold on January 7). So, of the 750 units we sold on January 8, 500 units came from the lot purchased on January 4 at $35 each. This finishes off that lot. The oldest inventory that we now have left is the 1,250 units purchased on January 5 at $40 each. The sale on January 8 was 750 units, of which 500 came from the January 4 purchase. We thus need 250 units from the January 5 purchase.

500 at $35 =	$17,500
250 at $40 =	$10,000
Total	$27,500

The entry to record the sale on January 8 is:

1/08/02	Cost of goods sold	27,500	
	Inventory		27,500
	To record the sale of 750 units that cost:		
	(500 × $35) + (250 × $40)		

The last sale takes place on January 10, when we sell 1,000 units. There are no units left from the January 4 purchase, and there are 1,000 units left from the January 5 purchase (1,250 − 250). The sale on January 10 exhausts the January 5 purchase. The entry to record the sale on January 10 is:

```
1/10/02    Cost of goods sold          40,000
           Inventory                              40,000
           To record the sale of 1,000 units that cost $40
```

The amount debited to Inventory was $169,000, and the amount removed from Inventory and transferred to Cost of goods sold was $85,000 ($17,500 + $27,500 + $40,000). The balance we are left with in the Inventory account is therefore $84,000 ($169,000 − $85,000). Fortunately, there is a way to check our work. The FIFO assumption says that the units sold came from the units received earliest by the company. Therefore, the units remaining in inventory came from the units that were the last to be received. We have 2,000 units left (4,250 purchased less 2,250 sold), and these would all be from the last purchase of 2,000 units at $42 each. Therefore, the ending inventory balance should be 2,000 units times a price of $42, which equals $84,000. So we did it correctly.

A complete list of the Inventory and Cost of goods sold entries involved in this example is as follows:

```
1/04/02    Inventory                   35,000
              Accounts payable            35,000
           To record purchase of inventory
           (1,000 units × $35)

1/05/02    Inventory                   50,000
              Accounts payable            50,000
           To record purchase of inventory
           (1,250 units × $40)

1/07/02    Cost of goods sold          17,500
              Inventory                       17,500
           To record the sale of 500 units that cost $35
```

1/08/02   Cost of goods sold   27,500
            Inventory   27,500
            To record the sale of 500 units that cost
            $35 each and 250 units that cost $40 each

1/09/02   Inventory   84,000
            Accounts payable   84,000
            To record purchase of inventory
            (2,000 units × $40)

1/10/02   Cost of goods sold   40,000
            Inventory   40,000
            To record the sale of 1,000 units that cost $40

When using the FIFO method, start at the top of the list and work down to figure out the Cost of the goods sold, and start at the bottom of the list and work up to figure out the value of the remaining Inventory.

Last-In, First-Out

As you can imagine, LIFO is the opposite of FIFO. With LIFO, we assume that the last units purchased are the first goods sold. In some cases, this might even approximate the physical flow of the goods. If we sold firewood, for example, we might stack the wood in a storage area. All new inventory would be stacked on top. When someone wants to make a purchase, we take the wood off the top, thereby giving the purchaser the units that were the last in.

The sale on January 7 is assumed to have come from the 1,250 units that cost $40 each (the last ones in). The entry to record this is:

```
1/07/02   Cost of goods sold       20,000
          Inventory                          20,000
          To record the sale of 500 units that cost $40
```

The sale on January 8 is assumed to have come from the remainder of the 1,250 units (thereby depleting that inventory). The entry to record this sale is:

```
1/08/02   Cost of goods sold       30,000
          Inventory                          30,000
          To record the sale of 750 units that cost $40
```

The last sale is assumed to have come from the purchase of 2,000 units at $42. The last sale was 1,000 units, and the entry is:

```
1/10/02   Cost of goods sold       42,000
          Inventory                          42,000
          To record the sale of 1,000 units that cost $42
```

When all is said and done, we debited $169,000 to Inventory for the purchases (this is the same no matter what cost flow assumption is chosen). With LIFO, we transferred $92,000 ($20,000 + $30,000 + $42,000) to Cost of goods sold, leaving $77,000 as the balance in the Inventory account. As with FIFO, we can check our answer.

There are 2,000 units left. Under LIFO, the units sold are the last ones in; therefore, the units remaining in inventory were the first ones in. The first units in were the January 4 purchase of 1,000 units at $35, for a total of $35,000. The January 5 purchase was used up, so the remaining units came from the 2,000 units purchased on January 9 at $42 each. There are

1,000 units left from this group, so 1,000 at $42 equals $42,000. Our calculation of what the balance in the Inventory account should be is $35,000 plus $42,000, which equals $77,000. We did it right again.

When a company elects to use the LIFO method, it is required to also keep track of what the balance in Inventory would be if it had used the FIFO method. This is disclosed in the footnotes to the financial statements. This is a fair amount of work and something of a burden, but if the company chooses to use LIFO, it should be aware of this requirement.

Weighted Average

The weighted average cost flow assumption uses the weighted average of all units purchased. Each time a purchase is made, a new weighted average is computed. The first purchase occurs on January 4. We get 1,000 units at a cost of $35 each. The total value of the order is $35,000. To find the weighted average, we take the total balance of Inventory and divide by the total number of units.

Total inventory value	$35,000
Total units	1,000
Weighted average	$ 35.00

When the purchase on January 5 is made, we need to recompute the weighted average. We do this by taking the total value of the purchases ($35,000 + $50,000) and dividing by the total number of units (1,000 + 1,250):

Total inventory value	$85,000
Total units	2,250
Weighted average	$ 37.78

We do not need to recompute the weighted average when sales are made; only when purchases take place. The sale of 500 units on January 7 is assumed to be at a cost of $37.78. The entry is:

1/07/02	Cost of goods sold	18,890	
	Inventory		18,890
	To record the sale of 500 units at a cost of		
	$37.78		

The sale of 750 units on January 8 also occurs at $37.78 per unit. The total cost is $28,335. The entry is:

1/08/02	Cost of goods sold	28,335	
	Inventory		28,335
	To record the sale of 750 units at a cost of		
	$37.78		

On January 9, a purchase of 2,000 units is made at a cost of $42 each. At this time, the inventory is 1,000 units (1,000 + 1,250 − 500 − 750) at an average cost of $37.78. To this we add 2,000 units at $42 each and recalculate the weighted average as follows:

1,000 units at $37.78 equals	$37,780
2,000 units at $42.00 equals	84,000
Total inventory value	121,780
Total number of units	3,000
Weighted average	$ 40.59

The last sale of 1,000 units occurs at the weighted average price of $40.59 each. The entry to record the cost of the sale is:

1/10/02   Cost of goods sold   40,590
             Inventory   40,590
             To record the sale of 1,000 units at a cost of
             $40.59

The balance remaining in inventory is the $169,000 we started with less the amounts transferred to Cost of goods sold:

Inventory purchases	$169,000
Less: Amounts transferred	
Jan. 8	18,890
Jan. 9	28,335
Jan. 10	40,590
Ending inventory balance	$ 81,185

As in the other situations, we can check to make sure we did it correctly. There are 2,000 units left in inventory at the weighted average cost of $40.59.

Units remaining	2,000
Weighted average cost	$ 40.59
Ending inventory balance	$81,180

Again, we did it right, since the proof equals the balance in the account (there is a $5 rounding difference).

Things to Keep in Mind

Inventory represents goods on hand that will be sold in the future (hopefully the very near future). When the goods are sold, the cost is transferred from Inventory to Cost of goods sold. Specific identification is a method that directly associates the amount it cost to acquire the particular item sold (the amount put into Inventory) with the cost transferred to Cost of goods sold.

In many (even most) cases it is not possible to directly track when an item from a particular shipment is sold. We therefore need to select a cost flow assumption. There are three choices of cost flow assumption: FIFO, LIFO, and weighted average. FIFO and LIFO assume that the goods sold were either the first ones purchased (FIFO) or the last ones purchased (LIFO). With the weighted average method, a new weighted average cost is calculated every time a purchase is made, and this weighted average cost is used to transfer the cost from Inventory to Cost of goods sold.

Why would a company choose one method over another? In a period in which prices are either rising or falling, we can make certain statements about how each inventory cost flow assumption would affect the financial statements. FIFO transfers the cost of the earliest inventory items to Cost of goods sold. In periods of rising prices, these will be the lowest-cost items. Therefore, the amount transferred to Cost of goods sold is less. Cost of goods sold is a reduction of income, and since it is lower, the use of FIFO produces a greater net income. It also leads to a higher value of ending inventory, since the goods that remain are the ones that were purchased last, at the higher prices.

Using LIFO in a period of rising prices has the opposite effect. LIFO transfers to Cost of goods sold the cost of the items that were purchased last, which are the higher-priced ones. Higher Cost of goods sold translates to lower net income. It also means that the Inventory account is lower. Why would a company choose to have a lower net income? To reduce taxes. Taxes are a real cash outlay and a real expense. Sometimes companies prefer to show less net income and pay less tax. The weighted-average method falls between FIFO and LIFO in both periods of rising prices and periods of falling prices.

Another consideration is what method other companies in your industry use. Some managers will opt to be consistent with other companies in their industry because analysts will compare them to these companies, and using similar methods makes comparison easier. If there is a predominant method, companies sometimes select that method without giving much thought to other considerations. Finally, there is the consideration of the recordkeeping involved. LIFO requires the company to also keep records as if it used FIFO. Some companies do not want the extra burden related to adopting the LIFO method.

9

Prepaid Expenses

Up to this point, we have recorded expenses by debiting the expense account and crediting either Cash or Accounts payable. Sometimes when we make a payment for an expense, however, the expense is not used up right away. An example of this would be paying for a two-year insurance policy. The only part of this payment that should be shown as an expense is the amount relating to the months that have gone by. Let's say the premium for the two-year policy was $2,400 and we paid this amount in October. The policy runs from November 2002 through October 2004 (24 months). When we prepare the financial statements for the year ended December 31, 2002, the portion of the premium that goes from Prepaid expenses to Insurance expense has to be computed.

When we make a payment that covers a period that extends beyond the financial statement date, we debit the payment to Prepaid expenses (the credit goes to Cash or Accounts payable). In our example, the entry would be:

10/01/02	Prepaid expenses	2,400
	Cash	2,400

To record payment for a two-year insurance policy

At the end of the year (December 31, 2002), an analysis of how much of this two-year premium has been used up has to be done. Since the policy starts in November, two months have been used up (November and December). We would move two months of premium from Prepaid expenses (an asset) to Insurance expense (an expense). We would calculate how much to move by using a proration. We paid $2,400 for 24 months of coverage; therefore each month cost $100. Since two months have been used up, 2 times $100 (or $200) needs to be transferred. The entry is:

12/31/02	Insurance expense	200
	Prepaid expenses	200

To record the portion of insurance expired

Another common example of a Prepaid expense is subscriptions. The process of reviewing the Prepaid expenses account to see if any part of it should be transferred to expense is covered in Chapter 18.

10

Other Receivables

The most common receivables are Accounts receivable. Accounts receivable arise when a company makes a sale on credit and thus is owed money by the customer. There are other types of receivables as well. Instead of making a sale, a company can make a loan to another entity and get a *note* in return. A note is a formal legal document that sets forth the terms of the loan.

The note should say who is making the loan (the *maker*), who is getting the loan (the *debtor*), the *date* of the loan, the amount of the loan (also called the *face amount* or the *principal*), when the loan needs to be repaid (the *maturity date*) or the *term* of the loan (usually expressed in days or months), and the *interest rate*.

Loan Term

If the loan expresses the term in months, the maturity date is the same day as the loan is made, after counting the number of months specified. If the loan is made January 5 and it is for three months, then the loan comes due April 5.

When the term is expressed in days, you actually have to count the days. Let's say a loan is made on January 5 for 60 days. You start counting with the day after the loan is made and continue counting until you have counted 60 days.

January 6–31	26 days
February	28 days (54 days total, so far)
March	6 days (60 days total)

The 60-day loan made on January 5 matures on March 6. If we made a two-month loan on January 5, it would mature on March 5.

Interest

Calculating the amount of interest is very straightforward. There are three items needed to figure out the amount of interest: the principal, the interest rate, and the period of time that the loan is outstanding. The principal is the amount of the loan (the face value). The interest rate is usually expressed as an annual figure. The period of time that the loan is outstanding is expressed in either days or months.

Let's say that we issued a $1,000 note at a rate of 12 percent for 90 days. The way to calculate the interest is:

Face × Interest Rate × Period of Time Outstanding
1,000 × 12%   × 90/365 = $29.59

Some people use 360 days as the number of days in the year. The note should specify what the basis should be, since it affects the calculation of interest. In general, it is acceptable to use either. In this example, using a 360-day year would result in interest expense of $30.00.

Entries

When the loan matures (comes due), the maker expects to receive payment of the principal plus the interest. The entries involved in the process of issuing a note are:

To record the purchase of a $1,000, 90-day note at 12 percent on January 5, 2002:

1/05/02	Note receivable	1,000	
	Cash		1,000
	To record issuance of note		

To record payment of the note at maturity on April 5, 2002:

4/05/02	Cash	1,029.59	
	Note receivable		1,000.00
	Interest income		29.59
	To record payment of note		

In addition to notes, a company may also purchase bonds or loans. Loans, bonds, and notes are all very similar. The difference among them is the underlying legal document that formalizes the transaction. Typically, loans and notes have a shorter term than bonds. The accounting is similar, differing only in what we title the account.

Keep in mind that this chapter is concerned with the company purchasing the security. The company that issues the security is called the *issuer,* and its accounting will parallel ours (we debited Notes receivable; they will credit Notes payable, etc.). In Chapter 15, we will be the issuer.

CHAPTER 11

Fixed Assets

Fixed assets are also called plant assets or plant, property, and equipment. All of these terms are synonymous. Three common traits of these assets are that they are used in the operation of the business, they last more than one year, and they usually are fairly expensive.

Fixed assets are recorded at cost. All the amounts necessary to get the asset ready for use are included as part of the cost. These amounts commonly include the cost of the item, sales tax, and delivery and installation costs. There will be separate fixed-asset accounts for Land, Land improvements, Leasehold improvements, Buildings, Equipment, Machinery, Furniture, Fixtures, and Vehicles. Some companies choose to combine some of these accounts, using accounts such as Machinery and equipment or Furniture and fixtures.

The initial one-time payments related to the purchase of the asset are part of its cost. Ongoing payments for maintaining and operating the asset are not part of its cost. As an example, let's take the acquisition of a car. This is something a lot of people can relate to. Here is the information pertaining to the purchase price agreed to with the dealer:

Auto cost	$24,500
Taxes	1,960
Title	500
Dealer prep	500
Total	$27,460

The entry to record the acquisition of the auto (assuming that cash was paid) is:

XX/XX/XX	Vehicle	27,460	
	Cash		27,460
	To record acquisition of auto		

Sometimes financing is involved. Suppose the company paid $2,000 and got a loan for the rest of the purchase price. The entry would be:

XX/XX/XX	Vehicle	27,460	
	Cash		2,000
	Loan payable		25,460
	To record acquisition of auto		

A year later, the company pays $45 to re-register the car with the motor vehicle department. This amount is charged to an expense, not to the asset account Vehicles. Routine repairs and maintenance are charged to expense as well. However, if the company needed to replace the engine, which costs $2,000, that amount would be added to the asset account, not charged to expense. The entry to record the new engine would be:

```
XX/XX/XX    Vehicle                    2,000
              Cash                            2,000
            To record acquisition of new engine
```

A general guideline is that any expenditure that lengthens the life of the asset or improves its productivity or efficiency, and that lasts more than a year, gets added to the asset account, whereas any expenditure that is routine and ordinary in nature gets charged to expense.

Land

The amount in the Land account is the cost of raw land or, if land with a building on it is acquired, the portion of the total purchase price that is allocated to the land. If there is a building on the land that is intended to be razed (knocked down) once the land is acquired, the cost of razing the building is added to the cost of the land. In addition, the cost of getting the land ready for its intended use is added to the Land account.

Land Improvements

Land improvements are things done to the land that have a discrete useful life. These can include fencing, grading (changing the slope of the land), paving, and lighting. Land improvements are kept in an account separate from that of the land on which they sit.

Leasehold Improvements

Leasehold improvements are improvements done to property that the company leases.

Buildings

Buildings can be built or purchased. If a building is built, the cost includes the architect's fees, payments to contractors, and the cost of permits and inspections. If the building is purchased, the amount debited to the asset account includes the cost of the building, legal fees, survey costs, title insurance costs, and most costs paid at closing. Most repairs done to the building will be either charged to expense (for the usual, ordinary items) or set up as a separate asset account (such as a roof replacement or the purchase of a new boiler).

Equipment and Machinery

Equipment and machinery (sometimes they are kept in separate accounts) are those major tools and implements used in the operation of the business. For a service company, these can include computers, copiers, telephone systems, and any electronic gear. For a manufacturing company, they include such things as drill presses, lathe machines, sanders, and other large tools.

Furniture

Furniture includes items such as desks, chairs, file cabinets, lamps, couches, and tables.

Fixtures

Fixtures are items such as store lighting, signage, and display cases.

Vehicles

Vehicles are the cars, trucks, and other transportation equipment that are owned by the company.

Depreciation

When a company buys a building or a piece of equipment, the cost is *capitalized,* or set up in an asset account. One of the principles of accounting is matching revenue with expense. If we own a building that is rented out as a store and offices, then it is involved in the production of revenue. How do we match the cost of the building to the revenue? A common denominator among all fixed assets is that they last longer than one year, and therefore they participate in generating many years' revenue. That is where the concept of depreciation comes in—taking the cost of an asset and spreading it over the years that will benefit from having the asset.

There are two common methods for depreciating an asset, straight-line and declining-balance. To calculate depreciation, three things have to be known: the cost of the asset, the method used to depreciate it, and its useful life. There is also a concept known as salvage value, but salvage value is used so infrequently in practice that we won't include it in our illustrations.

Straight-Line Depreciation

Straight-line depreciation is simple to understand: You take the cost of the asset and divide it by the asset's useful life.

Let's say a building cost $500,000 and its useful life is 25 years (40 is the maximum that we use). The annual depreciation will be $500,000 divided by 25, or $20,000 per year. The entry to record the depreciation is:

```
12/31/XX  Depreciation expense                        20,000
               Accumulated depreciation—Building    20,000
           To record annual depreciation on building
```

Each asset account will have its own associated accumulated depreciation account. The accumulated depreciation account has a credit balance, and since the account it is associated with is an asset account, it is a contra account, in this case a contra-asset account.

On the Balance Sheet, it is common practice to list each fixed asset separately and to group the accumulated depreciation accounts. The composition of the accumulated depreciation accounts is shown in the notes.

An example of the fixed asset section of the Balance Sheet is as follows:

Land	$100,000
Building	500,000
Equipment	50,000
Furniture	25,000
Fixtures	15,000
	690,000
Less: Accumulated depreciation	190,000
Net fixed assets	$500,000

The notes would have the following footnote about the components of the Accumulated depreciation shown on the Balance Sheet:

"Accumulated depreciation in the amount of $190,000 consists of the following:

Building	$151,000
Equipment	20,000
Furniture	10,000
Fixtures	9,000
Total accumulated depreciation	$190,000"

Notice that there is no accumulated depreciation for land. This is because, based on accounting convention, land is not depreciated.

Declining-Balance Depreciation

Declining-balance depreciation is a method of accelerated depreciation. That means that you have more depreciation in the early years of the asset's life and less in the later years. This fits the matching principle: Since assets are usually more productive in their early years, they will be involved in producing more revenue during those years, and therefore more of the cost should be charged to expense during those years.

The common types of declining balance are 125 percent, 150 percent, 175 percent, and 200 percent;. 200 percent declining-balance is also called double-declining-balance. All the methods work the same way; the only difference is the percentage applied.

The application of the declining-balance method starts with the useful life. Let's say we are depreciating a piece of equipment that cost $30,000 and has a five-year useful life. The first step is to take the useful life and turn it into a percentage. If we are depreciating an asset over five years, we take one-fifth each year, or 20 percent. In the declining-balance method, we multiply that 20 percent by the percentage indicating the type of declining-balance depreciation we are using (125 percent, 150 percent, and so on). Let's say we are using double-declining-balance (200 percent). The first year's depreciation would be $12,000. We get that $12,000 by taking the 20 percent (which is the straight-line depreciation rate) and applying our declining-balance percentage (200 percent). Multiplying 20 percent by 200 percent produces 40 percent. This 40 percent is multiplied by the book value of the asset. The book value is the cost of the asset less the accumulated depreciation taken on it. In this example, $30,000 times 40 percent equals $12,000.

In the second year, we take the book value of the asset and multiply it by the same 40 percent. In year 2 the book value is $18,000 (the cost of $30,000 less the depreciation taken, $12,000), and multiplying that times 40 percent equals $7,200.

In year 3, we take the book value of $10,800 (the cost of $30,000 less the depreciation taken of $12,000 and $7,200) and multiply it by 40 percent to get the third year's depreciation of $4,320. Figure 11-1 shows the annual calculation of depreciation.

When a declining-balance method of depreciation is used,

FIGURE 11-1			
Year	Book Value	Rate	Depreciation
1	30,000	40%	12,000
2	18,000	40%	7,200
3	10,800	40%	4,320
4	6,480	50%	3,240
5	3,240	100%	3,240

it is customary to switch to straight-line depreciation toward
the end of the asset's life. In the example shown in Figure 11-1,
this switch was made in the fourth year. The book value (the
amount remaining to be depreciated) is divided in half (since
two years of the useful life remain), and half of it is taken as
depreciation in each of the next two years. If the switch had
been made in year 3, we would have divided the remaining
book value by 3 (since three years would have remained) to
calculate the remaining annual depreciation.

What happens if a company decides that it made a mistake
in the depreciable life? Let's take an example, this time using
straight-line depreciation. Let's say that an asset cost $50,000
and is being depreciated over five years. Using straight-line
depreciation, the annual depreciation will be $10,000. At the
beginning of the fourth year, the company decides that the
asset has another four years of life. This is considered a change
in estimate. When a company changes an estimate, the change
is made currently and into the future. Past information is not
restated.

By the beginning of the fourth year, the company would
have taken $30,000 of depreciation expense (three years times
$10,000 a year). The book value of the asset is thus $20,000
(the cost of $50,000 less accumulated depreciation of $30,000).
Since there are still four years of useful life left, the company
would take the book value and divide it evenly over the remaining four years. The annual depreciation will now be
$5,000 ($20,000 divided by four years).

What would happen if the company were to decide that the
asset would not last as long as it had originally thought? Let's
go back to our example and modify it slightly. The asset cost
$50,000, and the company thought it would last five years. At
the beginning of the third year, the company realizes that the

asset will last only two more years. At the beginning of the third year, the book value is $30,000 (the cost of $50,000 less accumulated depreciation of $20,000). Since there are only two years of useful life left, the company should take the book value and divide it over the remaining life. This will change the annual depreciation to $15,000 for the next two years ($30,000 divided by 2).

Partial-Year Depreciation

In our examples, we have assumed that the company acquires the asset on the first day of the year. This is seldom the case. How do you handle acquisitions during the year? There are two methods. The first is a strict proration based on how much of the year is left. If you acquired the asset on February 1, you would calculate depreciation using whichever method you have selected, and then take eleven-twelfths of that amount during the first year. As you can predict, there will be a partial year of depreciation in the last year as well. So if the asset has a five-year useful life, there will a little depreciation left in year 6 (the one-twelfth remaining from the first year, essentially).

The other way to handle the initial-year depreciation is to have a policy. This policy might state that no matter what the actual date of acquisition is, the company will take one-half or one-fourth of a full year's depreciation. Both methods (proration and policy) are acceptable, as long as the method chosen is consistently applied.

Retirement

If a company keeps an asset until it is fully depreciated, then gets rid of it (let's say the company throws it out), this is called a *retirement*. The entry for a retirement removes both the asset account and the accumulated depreciation account. Let's go back to our example. Let's say the asset cost $50,000 and was fully depreciated (meaning that Accumulated depreciation was $50,000). The journal entry to retire the asset we would be:

XX/XX/XX	Accumulated depreciation	50,000	
	Asset		50,000
	To record retirement of asset		

If the asset is retired in the fourth year, when the accumulated depreciation is $30,000, the entry to retire the asset is:

XX/XX/XX	Accumulated depreciation	30,000	
	Asset		50,000
	Needed to balance	20,000	
	To record retirement of asset		

You can see that we need a debit to balance the journal entry. The debit we need is a special type of expense—a loss. We would title the account "Loss on retirement."

Asset Sale

Another possibility is that we sell the asset. Let's go back to our retirement example. Instead of being retired during the third year, the asset is sold for $40,000. The entry is:

XX/XX/XX	Accumulated depreciation	20,000	
	Asset		50,000
	Cash	40,000	
	Needed to balance		10,000
	To record sale of asset		

In this case, we need a credit to balance the journal entry. This is a special type of revenue—a gain. We would title the account "Gain on sale of asset."

Let's say we sold the asset for $20,000 instead of $40,000. The entry would be:

XX/XX/XX	Accumulated depreciation	20,000	
	Asset		50,000
	Cash	20,000	
	Loss on Sale	10,000	
	To record sale of asset		

The easiest way to make the entry (and to always get it right) is to debit the Accumulated depreciation account for the depreciation taken, and then credit the asset account (for the asset's cost). Debit anything that was received (if the asset was sold or traded). If you still need a debit to balance the account, you have a loss; if you need a credit to balance the account, you have a gain.

When you are selling or trading in the asset, you have to remember to take a partial year's depreciation in the last year (prorated to the day of disposal or based on the company's policy, such as always taking one-half year's depreciation in the year of disposal). The examples we have used so far did not include depreciation in the year of disposal. After taking the partial depreciation in the year of disposal, we would then apply the rules given earlier. Here's an example to illustrate. Let's say a piece of equipment costs $60,000 and has a six-year life. The Accumulated depreciation account has a balance of $10,000. The company uses straight-line depreciation. On March 1, the company sells the asset for $48,000.

The first step is to compute depreciation from January 1 to

March 1 (the partial year's depreciation in the year of sale or trade-in). The period from January 1 to March 1 is two months. As a portion of a year, that turns out to be $2/12$ or $1/6$. Annual depreciation for a full year would be $10,000 (the cost of $60,000 divided by 6 years). Prorating the $10,000 gives the final year's depreciation as $1,667 (computed by taking $10,000 and multiplying by $1/6$). The entry to record this partial year's depreciation is:

XX/XX/XX Depreciation expense   1,667
            Accumulated depreciation—Equipment   1,667
            To record depreciation to day of sale

Now apply the rule given earlier:

1. Debit the accumulated depreciation, which is now $11,667 ($10,000 + 1,667).

2. Credit the asset account, which is $60,000.

3. Debit anything received, which is $48,000.

4. If a debit is needed to balance the journal entry, then it is a loss; if a credit is needed to balance the entry, then it is a gain. Let's put all the entries into the equation and see what we need:

03/01/02 Accumulated depreciation—Equipment   11,667
          Cash   48,000
            Equipment   60,000
          Loss on sale of equipment   333
          To record sale of equipment

12

Intangible Assets

Intangible assets are assets that have no physical substance. In general, intangible assets are rights or privileges of some sort. The assets that are typically classified as intangible are patents, copyrights, franchises, trademarks, and trade names. It's important to remember that the cost recorded is not the value of the intangible asset, but only the amount spent to acquire it. Let's go back a hundred years or so in time and pretend we are Coca-Cola. We come up with the name Coca-Cola (and Coke), and we think it is kind of catchy, so we decide to use it for our product. We pay a lawyer to file the legal papers necessary to protect the name. Let's say that the cost of filing the papers and paying the lawyer comes to a total of $1,000. That would be the amount we would capitalize as the asset (capitalizing is another way of saying recording). Even though the name has grown in value in the ensuing hundred years, we show only the amount we paid to acquire it.

We add to the asset account any amounts that we pay to

defend our interests, such as paying a lawyer to sue a company that uses a name that is too similar to ours. If we were to purchase the name from another company, we can record as the asset any amounts we paid to acquire the name. So if we can convince Coca-Cola to sell us the name for $1 billion, that is the amount we would record as an intangible asset (even though Coke's accounting records say that the carrying value of the asset is $1,000).

If this were a fixed asset (for example, plant, property, or equipment), we would depreciate the asset. We don't depreciate intangible assets; instead, we use a process called *amortization*. Functionally, amortization is very similar to depreciation. Since intangible assets are rights, often there are legal limits on how long we possess the rights. That's why we say that the amortization period for intangible assets is the shorter of:

- The legal life

- The useful life

- Forty years

The legal life of a patent is seventeen years from the date the patent was issued. The legal life of a copyright is seventy years from the year the author dies. The legal life of a franchise is determined by the franchise agreement.

It is common practice to record the amortization in the asset account, instead of using a separate Accumulated amortization account. My preference is to use a separate Accumulated amortization account when a company has multiple intangible assets in the same account (for example, when there are three patents included in the Patents account). This makes it easier to know how much was paid for each asset and to associate the amortization taken should an item be sold. If the items are always held until they are fully amortized, then it really doesn't matter.

An example will illustrate the entries. Let's say it costs $17,000 to get a patent filed and granted. The patent is granted January 1. We believe that its useful life is twenty-five years. To record the patent, the entry is:

```
1/01/XX    Patent                      17,000
              Cash                              17,000
           To record acquisition of patent
```

To record the annual amortization, the entry is:

```
12/31/XX   Patent expense              1,000
              Patent                            1,000
           To record annual amortization
```

The annual amortization is calculated by taking the cost ($17,000) and dividing it by the lesser of the useful life (twenty-five years), the legal life (seventeen years), or forty years. The lesser of the three lives is seventeen years. Therefore, the cost ($17,000) divided by the amortization life (17) equals the annual amortization ($1,000). Posting the entries to the general ledger account would result in an account balance of $16,000, as shown in Figure 12-1.

If the asset and the amortization are kept in separate accounts, then the posting of the entries results in the situation shown in Figure 12-2.

FIGURE 12-1	
Patent	
17,000	1,000
16,000	

FIGURE 12-2			
Patent		**Accumulated Amortization**	
17,000			1,000

CHAPTER 13

Liabilities

Liabilities are the things that you owe. Liabilities require the future sacrifice of assets. In most of the transactions in our examples, we have been assuming that we paid cash. In business, however, credit is often used rather than paying with cash or a check. If we purchase something on credit, the credit will be to Accounts payable rather than to Cash.

Like assets, liabilities are classified as current or noncurrent (also called long-term). Current liabilities are those liabilities that are expected to be satisfied within the next twelve months (the next year). Noncurrent liabilities are those liabilities that are not expected to be satisfied within the next twelve months.

In some cases, a portion of a liability will be paid within the next year and another portion will not be. A good example of this is a mortgage. A mortgage is a loan secured by real estate that usually has a long payment term. Payments are made every month, so there is a portion of the mortgage that will be paid within the next year. The balance of the mortgage therefore has to be split into two pieces: the piece that will be paid during the next year and the remainder that will be paid after the next year (the current piece and the long-term piece). The piece that will be paid next year is shown with the current liabilities and is called Current portion of long-term debt or something similar.

Unearned Revenue

Any account whose title includes the word *payable* is a liability. In addition, there are some liabilities whose titles do not include the word *payable*. Unearned revenue is a liability. Unearned revenue represents money that has been paid to the company for work that has not yet been performed or goods that remain to be shipped. It cannot be considered revenue until the work has been done (or the goods have been shipped). Every time work that was prepaid is done, a portion of the unearned revenue is moved to Revenue (since it has now been earned). Let's assume that on June 27, 2002, we were paid $25,000 for work that we will perform in the future. The entry to record the receipt of the $25,000 is:

6/27/02	Cash	25,000	
	Unearned revenue		25,000
	To record cash receipt		

Now let's say that during July we perform $10,000 of the work. The entry is:

7/31/02	Unearned revenue	10,000	
	Revenue		10,000
	To record work performed		

We will keep working off the balance in the Unearned revenue account. When we have performed all the work anticipated by the original payment ($25,000), we will either send the client a bill for another prepayment or bill the client as we perform work on its behalf.

Accrued Expenses

We usually record an expense when a bill (also called an invoice) is received. Expenses that are recorded before any bill has been received are called *accrued expenses*. Companies will record accrued expenses in order to make sure that their financial statements are accurate. Financial statements are prepared on the *accrual basis,* which means that cash does not have to change hands in order for something to be recorded. The items that will be included in accrued expenses are discussed in detail in Chapter 18.

Current liabilities are listed in the order in which they are expected to be satisfied. The ones that will be paid first are listed first. Noncurrent liabilities are grouped by type (Loans payable, Bonds payable, Notes payable, and so on). The footnotes will usually explain the components of the noncurrent liabilities (the basic terms, maturities, interest rates, and so on).

Accounts Payable

Accounts payable is a frequently used account—it is used whenever a company buys anything on credit. This might be inventory, office supplies, or equipment. When the merchandise is received, the company debits the appropriate account for whatever is received (Inventory if inventory was received; Office supplies if paper clips were received, and so on) and credits Accounts payable. When payment is made, the company debits Accounts payable (which reduces the amount owed—since the company is making a payment, it no longer owes that amount) and credits Cash. Let's use another example.

On August 23, 2002, the company receives office supplies purchased on credit:

8/23/02	Office supplies	1,250	
	Accounts payable		1,250
	To record receipt of office supplies purchased on credit		

On September 15, 2002, the company sends its payment for the office supplies:

9/15/02   Accounts payable   1,250
          Cash   1,250
          To record payment on account

Many companies offer their customers an incentive to get them to pay their bills faster. This is called a *cash discount*. If the selling company offers a cash discount, the discount will be specified on the invoice, usually with a notation that reads something like "2/10, n/30." That notation is read, "2 percent discount if paid within 10 days; otherwise full payment expected in 30 days." The terms can be anything a company wants to offer. The company simply adjusts the notation to reflect the terms it is offering, such as:

1/10, n/30—1 percent discount if paid within 10 days; otherwise full payment is due in 30 days

1/15, n/20—1 percent discount if paid within 15 days; otherwise full payment is due in 20 days

2/10, n/20—2 percent discount if paid within 10 days; otherwise full payment is due in 20 days

For the seller, the cash discount is called a *sales discount*. If the discount is taken on a purchase, it may be called a *purchase discount*.

If a company takes a discount, it doesn't have to send quite as much money as it has recorded as the amount of the payable. If we ordered office supplies and the bill was for $1,000, the entry to record the purchase is:

```
XX/XX/XX    Office supplies              1,000
            Accounts payable                      1,000
            To record purchase of office supplies on credit
```

The invoice indicates that there is a 2 percent discount available for paying within 10 days. If we pay within 10 days, then we have to send only $980 [$1,000 – ($1,000 x 0.2)]. So the entry will be:

```
XX/XX/XX    Accounts payable             1,000
            Cash                                    980
            Needed to balance                        20
            To record payment on account
```

As you can see, we will need to credit some account for $20 in order to balance the account. What account should get the $20? We have a choice of which account to credit. If we took the discount on the purchase of an asset or the incurrence of an expense, we can reduce the asset or expense by using the credit to offset the original debit. The other option is to record the discount as revenue. If we want to record it as revenue, we should set up a discrete revenue account and call it something like Cash discounts, to distinguish it from the main revenue account. We also do not want to call the account Purchase dis-counts," as that title will be used in Chapter 17. Commonly, the credit will simply go to the original account debited. In this case, that account would be office supplies. The entry would therefore be:

```
XX/XX/XX    Accounts Payable             1,000
            Cash                                    980
            Office supplies                          20
            To record payment on account
```

15

Other Payables

The Accounts payable account is used when purchases are made on open credit, meaning that a company sends us goods (or provides us services) and bills us. There are other types of payables for which we most likely would not use Accounts payable. We would normally set up separate accounts to handle Interest payable, Rent payable, Taxes payable, Salaries payable, and Payroll taxes payable.

Interest Payable

At the end of each accounting period, the company should review the loans it has outstanding and see whether any interest has accrued during the period. On some loans, interest is paid only at the maturity of the loan. For accounting purposes, we want to show the interest that has been incurred through the financial statement date, even if the interest won't be paid for a while. Since the company has had the use of the money, we will make an adjustment to record the interest. The mechanics of the adjustment will be covered in Chapter 18.

Rent Payable

When rent is owed to the landlord, a separate, discrete payable is usually set up, rather than lumping the amount in with Accounts payable.

To record rent payable:

XX/XX/XX	Rent expense	3,500	
	Rent payable		3,500
	To record rent payable		

When the rent is paid:

XX/XX/XX	Rent payable	3,500	
	Cash		3,500
	To record payment of rent		

Taxes Payable

The tax return for a corporation that has a calendar year-end (December 31) is due March 15 of the following year. For the year ended December 31, the corporation may have generated net income, resulting in taxes that will have to be paid. These taxes are due on the income that was earned for the year ended December 31, even though they do not have to be paid until a couple of months later. We want to record the income tax in the period in which the income was generated (the matching principle again). To do this, we estimate what the tax will be when we finally get around to preparing the tax return. We then record the estimated tax with the following entry:

```
12/31/XX    Income tax expense       15,000
            Income tax payable           15,000
            To record income tax expense
```

When we file the tax return, we will send a check with it to pay the tax. The entry to record the check is:

```
XX/XX/XX    Income tax payable       15,000
            Cash                         15,000
            To record payment
```

Salaries Payable

More often than not, at the end of any accounting period, a company will owe its employees some wages. Think of yourself—did your last paycheck cover every day you worked right up to the pay date? We will talk about how to calculate the salaries payable in more detail in Chapter 18.

Payroll Taxes Payable

Whenever we accrue Salaries payable, we should also record the payroll taxes that we are responsible for paying (the employer's share) on those accrued salaries. This might include social security, Medicare, federal unemployment, state unemployment, workers' compensation, and disability. We record the items by debiting expense and crediting the liability (the payable). Let's say the accrued payroll totaled $100,000 and the relevant payroll taxes were social security (6.2 percent), Medicare (1.45 percent), federal unemployment (0.3 percent), and state unemployment (0.25 percent). An example of the journal entry is:

XX/XX/XX	Social security expense	6,200	
	Medicare expense	1,450	
	Federal unemployment tax	300	
	State unemployment tax	250	
	Payroll taxes payable		8,200
	To record payroll taxes on accrued payroll		

Another acceptable way to record the accrued payroll taxes is to use a separate journal entry for each item:

XX/XX/XX	Social security expense	6,200	
	Social security payable		6,200
	Medicare expense	1,450	
	Medicare payable		1,450
	Federal unemployment tax	300	
	Federal unemployment tax payable		300
	State unemployment tax	250	
	State unemployment tax payable		250
	To record payroll taxes on accrued payroll		

Yet another acceptable way to record the entry is to group all the items:

XX/XX/XX	Accrued payroll tax expense	8,200	
	Accrued payroll taxes payable		8,200
	To record payroll taxes on accrued payroll		

As with other payables, the entry to record the payment is to debit the payable and credit the Cash (checking) account.

16

Stockholders' Equity

The stockholders' equity section contains the capital contributed by the owners (also called shareholders or stockholders) and the earnings retained by the business (this account is called Retained earnings). On the Balance Sheet, the stockholders' equity section is divided into Contributed capital (capital put in by the owners) and Retained earnings. The contributed capital section contains an entry for each of the different types of stock the company has issued. Larger companies often issue two types of stock, common stock and preferred stock. Smaller companies will usually issue only common stock. In addition, there can be different types of common and preferred stock issued, with each type having unique privileges and benefits. Since the overwhelming majority of accountants will see only companies with a single class of common stock, we won't worry about all of the permutations that can happen. Let's look at an example of a stockholders' equity section of the Balance Sheet:

Stockholders' equity

Common stock (1,000,000 shares authorized, 500,000 shares issued and outstanding; par value of $0.01)	$ 5,000
Additional paid-in capital	495,000
Total contributed capital	500,000
Retained earnings	250,000
Total stockholders' equity	$750,000

Types of Stock

The most prevalent type of stock is common stock. Virtually every corporation issues common stock. Another type of stock that is popular, but to a much lesser extent, is preferred stock. There are some major differences between common and preferred stock. Common stock has voting rights, whereas preferred usually does not. Preferred stock has a preference in receiving dividends, which means that holders of common stock cannot be paid dividends unless the holders of preferred stock receive dividends.

The preferred stock often has additional benefits that make it act more like debt financing (such as a bond or a long-term note). There may be a stated percentage dividend rate (like an interest rate), there may be a rule that unpaid preferred stock dividends in any year are carried over and must be paid in the future before any dividends are paid to holders of common stock, and sometimes there is a conversion feature, meaning that a specified number of shares of preferred stock can be turned into (converted into) a stipulated number of common shares.

Common Stock

There are three major types of common stock:

- Par value

- No par value, but a stated value

- No par value

Par value is an arbitrary amount that is assigned to each share by the company. It has no relation to market value. Some jurisdictions levy taxes on the company based on the par value of the stock that has been issued. For this reason, many companies set the par value at a very low number (such as $0.01). Aside from its use in levying taxes, par value doesn't really serve any purpose.

Each company will file with the appropriate government body (usually the secretary of state in the state chosen for incorporation) a form called the Articles of Incorporation. In addition, the company will develop or buy another set of forms called the bylaws. These two sets of forms set the maximum number of shares the company may issue. This maximum is referred to as the *authorized* number of shares. The number of shares that have been sold to the public is called the number of shares *issued* (this can be the same as or less than the authorized number of shares).

Sometimes a company will go into the stock market and buy back some of the shares it had previously sold. There can be many reasons for this, such as an attempt to increase the stock price (when there are fewer shares outstanding, there is likely to be an increased demand for the stock), or perhaps a need to deliver stock to fulfill the company's obligation to a stock option or bonus plan. In any event, the stock repurchased by the company is called *treasury stock*. If there is a difference between the number of shares issued and the number of shares outstanding, it is because of treasury stock. Once the stock has been issued to the public, it is counted as issued, but if it is repurchased by the company and held as treasury stock, it is not included in the total of the stock outstanding. If a company has no treasury stock, then the figures for the issued and outstanding shares will be the same.

The following example will illustrate:

Example A

Number of shares authorized:	1,000,000 shares
Number of shares issued	500,000 shares
Number of treasury shares	0 shares

Therefore, the number of shares outstanding is 500,000 shares (500,000 shares issued – 0 shares in treasury).

Example B

Number of shares authorized	1,000,000 shares
Number of shares issued	500,000 shares
Number of treasury shares	200,000 shares

Therefore, the number of shares outstanding is 300,000 shares (500,000 shares issued – 200,000 shares in treasury).

Recording the Issuance

No matter whether the stock is par value, no par value but stated value, or no par value, the debit part of the transaction is always what the company receives. Usually this is cash. The credit side depends on the type of stock: whether it is par value, no par value but stated value, or no par value. If there is a par value or a stated value, there will be a credit to an account called Common stock for the number of shares issued multiplied by the par or stated value. If this is less than the amount received, there will be another credit to an account called Additional paid-in capital or sometimes Paid-in capital in excess of par.

So let us assume that a company has stock with a par value of $0.01. The company sells 100,000 shares on February 22, 2002, for a total price of $500,000. The entry would be:

2/22/02	Cash	500,000	(A)
	Common stock	1,000	(B)
	Additional paid-in capital	499,000	(C)
	To record issuance of stock		

(A) is the amount received

(B) is 100,000 times $0.01

(C) is the amount needed to balance the journal entry

If the stock issued were no par value, the entry would be:

2/22/02	Cash	500,000	
	Common stock	500,000	
	To record issuance of stock		

Treasury Stock

When a company buys its own stock in the open market, the entry is fairly straightforward. The company records the amount paid as a debit to Treasury stock (which is a reduction in the stockholders' equity section) and a credit to Cash for the amount paid for the stock.

Let's assume that on December 11, 2002, a company re-purchases 1,000 shares of its stock in the open market at a price of $4.00 per share. The entry to record the repurchase is:

12/11/02	Treasury stock	4,000	
	Cash		4,000
	To record purchase of treasury stock		

The stockholders' equity section of the balance sheet will appear as follows:

Stockholders' equity

Common stock (1,000,000 shares authorized, 500,000 issued, and 499,000 outstanding; par value of $0.01)	$ 5,000
Additional paid-in capital	495,000
Subtotal	500,000
Less: Treasury stock	4,000
Total contributed capital	496,000
Retained earnings	250,000
Total stockholders' equity	$746,000

Dividends

A company will generally issue dividends in the form of cash. Sometimes it will issue additional shares of its stock as a divi-dend (called a *stock dividend*) when it wants to issue a divi-dend but does not have the cash available for a cash dividend. Only the board of directors of a company may declare a dividend. Once a dividend is declared, it cannot be rescinded. The declaration of a dividend by the board of directors legally binds a company to pay that dividend.

There are many dates associated with the dividend. The date on which the dividend is declared by the board of directors is called the *declaration date*. On the declaration date, the company will make a journal entry to record the declaration of the dividend. It does this by debiting the Dividends account and recording a liability to pay the dividend. If there were 1,000,000 shares outstanding on December 18, 2002, and the board of directors declared a $1.00 dividend, the entry would be:

12/18/02	Dividends	1,000,000	
	Dividends payable		1,000,000
	To record the declaration of a dividend		
	(1,000,000 shares outstanding × $1.00 per		
	share)		

When the company declares the dividend, it will indicate a *record* date. Whoever owns the shares at the close of business on the record date will be entitled to the dividend. The record date enables the company to determine which shareholders get the dividend. Since the stock may be traded constantly, specifying the record date allows the public to know who will get the dividend. There is no journal entry needed on the record date.

The *payment* date is the date on which the company will send out the checks. Using the figures from the previous example, if the payment date is December 30, 2002, the entry will be:

```
12/30/02  Dividends payable        1,000,000
              Cash                             1,000,000
          To record the payment of dividends
```

No dividends are paid on treasury shares. If a company has treasury stock, these shares do not receive the dividend. If a company has 1,000,000 shares authorized, 500,000 issued, and 499,000 shares outstanding, then the declaration of a $1.00 per share dividend on December 19, 2002, would result in the following entry:

```
12/19/02  Dividends                      499,000
              Dividends payable             499,000
          To record declaration of dividends (499,000
          shares outstanding × $1.00 per share)
```

17

Merchandising Companies

The examples we have used so far have not discussed some characteristics that are specific to merchandising companies. Service companies offer a service to the public, such as accounting, bookkeeping, legal, architecture, billing, or consulting services. They derive their revenue by providing these services, with the sale of any merchandise being incidental to their operations. In contrast, merchandising companies get their revenue from the sale of merchandise or goods. They may get some revenue from the sale of services, but this is incidental to their operations.

The differences between service companies and merchandising companies are reflected in the financial statements. On the Balance Sheet, there is a minor difference: The merchandising company has inventory, and the service company does not. The bigger difference is on the Income Statement. The basic Income Statement used by service companies (also called the single-step Income Statement) is shown in Figure 17-1.

This type of Income Statement is called a single-step income statement because there is only one subtraction necessary to arrive at net income. Merchandising companies add at least one more step to the Income Statement. Since merchandising companies earn their revenue from the sale of products, the Income Statement needs to reflect both the money received from the sale of the goods and the cost of the goods that were sold. This interim step adds a subtotal called *gross profit.* Gross profit is the difference between revenue and the cost of goods sold (see Figure 17-2).

FIGURE 17-1

Jeffry Haber Company
Income Statement
For the Year Ended December 31, 2002

Revenues:	
Sales	$2,500,000
Interest income	24,000
Total revenue	$2,524,000
Expenses:	
Salaries	$1,875,000
Professional fees	240,000
Payroll taxes	187,500
Rent	110,000
Utilities	23,000
Office supplies	15,000
Office expense	12,000
Total expenses	$2,462,500
Net income	$61,500

FIGURE 17-2

Jeffry Haber Company
Income Statement
For the Year Ended December 31, 2002

Sales	$2,500,000
Cost of goods sold	1,650,000
Gross profit	$850,000

There are a lot more expenses to be accounted for on the Income Statement than those shown in Figure 17-2. The next section is called *operating expenses,* and it is broken down into selling expenses and general and administrative expenses (see Figure 17-3). Selling expenses are those expenses that are related to the selling of the merchandise. These include salaries of sales personnel, rent, utilities, repair and maintenance and other occupancy expenses, the cost of shipping the merchandise to customers, and other expenses that can be directly related to the sales function.

General and administrative expenses are those expenses that are related to the management of the company. These often include salaries for the executive, legal, human resources, and accounting departments; the related payroll taxes on those salaries; occupancy costs for the administrative offices; and general fees and costs paid by the company.

Often a company gets interest on its bank account (grouped with "other income") or pays interest on outstanding borrowings (grouped with "other expense"). These are usually grouped together after the operating income line. If the company has very few "other income" and "other expense"

FIGURE 17-3

Jeffry Haber Company
Income Statement
For the Year Ended December 31, 2002

Sales	$2,500,000
Cost of goods sold	1,650,000
Gross profit	$850,000

Operating expenses:
Selling expenses:
Salaries	125,000
Payroll taxes	34,000
Rent	12,000
Repair and maintenance	10,000
Real estate taxes	8,000
Freight out	6,500
Total selling expenses	195,500

General and administrative expenses:
Salaries	365,000
Payroll taxes	42,000
Rent	24,000
Repair and maintenance	10,000
Real extate taxes	7,000
Subscriptions	2,500
Professional fees	2,000
Total general and administrative expenses	452,500
Operating income	$202,000

---

items, it can group these items in one category (usually called "other income and other expense"), as shown in Figure 17-4.

If there are numerous items, there should be a separate section for each category, as shown in Figure 17-5.

When you add other income to operating income and sub-

FIGURE 17-4	
Other income and expense:	
Interest income	23,000
Interest expense	2,000
Total other income and expense	21,000

FIGURE 17-5	
Other income:	
Interest	23,000
Dividends	15,000
Gain on sale of asset	12,500
Total other income	50,500
Other expense:	
Interest	2,000
Loss on sale of asset	1,500
Total other expense	3,500
Total other income and expense	47,000

tract other expense from it, you get a figure called income before taxes. Subtracting income taxes yields the final line of the Income Statement, net income. Figure 17-6 shows the entire multistep Income Statement.

Perpetual Inventory System

If things were in fact this simple, it would not be so bad, but they can get more complicated. The multistep Income Statement illustrated is perfect, as long as the company uses a perpetual inventory system. In the perpetual inventory system, Cost of goods sold is recorded each time a sale is made (hence

---

FIGURE 17-6

Jeffry Haber Company
Income Statement
For the Year Ended December 31, 2002

Sales	$2,500,000
Cost of goods sold	1,650,000
Gross profit	$850,000

Operating expenses:
Selling expenses:

Salaries	125,000
Payroll taxes	34,000
Rent	12,000
Repair and maintenance	10,000
Real estate taxes	8,000
Freight out	6,500
Total selling expenses	195,500

General and administrative expenses:

Salaries	365,000
Payroll taxes	42,000
Rent	24,000
Repair and maintenance	10,000
Real extate taxes	7,000
Subscriptions	2,500
Professional fees	2,000
Total general and administrative expenses	452,500
Operating income	$202,000

Other income

Interest	23,000
Dividends	15,000
Gain on sale of asset	12,500
Total other income:	50,500

Other expense:

Interest	2,000
Loss on sale of asset	1,500
Total other expense	3,500
Total other income and expense	47,000
Income before taxes	$249,000
Income taxes	98,000
Net income	$151,000

the name *perpetual*). Let's say that 50 units were sold at $100 each. In addition, we know that those units cost us $55 each. There are really two entries we need to make for every sale:

1. Record the sale:

XX/XX/XX   Accounts receivable   5,000
              Sales   5,000
              To record the sale of 50 units at $100 each

2. Record the cost of the sale:

XX/XX/XX   Cost of goods sold   2,750
              Merchandise inventory   2,750
              To record the cost of sales of 50 units that cost
              $55 each

In order to use the perpetual inventory system, you have to have a sophisticated accounting system that utilizes scanning technology (unless you sell big things like houses or cars). Since many businesses now have access to this technology, the perpetual method is available to many companies.

With this system, whenever purchases are made, they are debited to an account called Merchandise inventory. When freight charges are paid to bring merchandise into the store or warehouse, these charges are also debited to Merchandise inventory. With the perpetual method, everything goes through Merchandise inventory.

Assuming that the freight charge was $150, the journal entry is:

```
XX/XX/XX   Merchandise inventory        150
              Accounts payable             150
           To record freight charges
```

If we return $1,000 of the purchases we made, the entry is:

```
XX/XX/XX   Accounts payable            1,000
              Merchandise inventory      1,000
           To record return of purchases for credit
```

Periodic Inventory System

The periodic inventory system assumes that a company is not able to record Cost of goods sold at the same time that the sale is recorded. Instead, the cost of goods sold will be recorded at the end of an accounting period. When we record the entries for a merchandising company that uses the periodic inventory system, such items as purchases, freight in, and purchase returns are all recorded in separate accounts. In the perpetual system, everything is recorded in the Merchandise inventory account, and in the periodic system, everything is recorded in separate accounts. Here are some examples of the periodic system in action:

Purchase 1,000 units at $45 each:

```
XX/XX/XX   Purchases                   45,000
              Accounts payable           45,000
           To record the purchase of 1,000 units at $45
           each
```

Sell 500 units at $80 each:

```
XX/XX/XX   Accounts receivable        40,000
              Sales                              40,000
              To record the sale of 500 units at $80 each
```

Return of 300 of the units purchased:

```
XX/XX/XX   Accounts payable           13,500
                 Purchase returns            13,500
              To record return of 300 units purchased (at $45
              each)
```

Customer returns 100 units:

```
XX/XX/XX   Sales returns              8,000
                 Accounts receivable         8,000
              To record returned sales (100 units at $80
              each)
```

The balances of these individual accounts will be shown on the multistep Income Statement and used to arrive at the Cost of goods sold figure.

Discounts for Early Payment

We can receive a discount for early payment from the company that is selling us merchandise. This is called a *purchase discount*. We can also offer our customers a discount if they pay us quickly. That is called a *sales discount*.

If we make purchases totaling $10,000, the entry to record the purchases would be (omitting explanations):

Perpetual system:

```
XX/XX/XXXX   Merchandise inventory      10,000
                Accounts payable            10,000
```

Periodic system:

```
XX/XX/XXXX   Purchases                  10,000
                Accounts payable            10,000
```

If the seller offers a 2 percent discount, and the date of our payment allows us to take the discount, the entry would be:

Perpetual system:

```
XX/XX/XXXX   Accounts payable           10,000
                Cash                         9,800
                Merchandise inventory          200
```

Periodic system:

```
XX/XX/XXXX   Accounts payable           10,000
                Cash                         9,800
                Purchase discounts             200
```

If we offer our customers a discount for early payment, it does not matter which system (perpetual or periodic) we use; the entry is the same. If we offer a 1 percent discount for early payment, and a customer takes the discount on a $1,000 payment, the entry would be:

XX/XX/XXXX	Cash	990
	Sales discounts	10
	Accounts receivable	1,000

Side-by-Side Comparison of the Periodic and Perpetual Systems

The following transactions will illustrate the journal entries required by the perpetual and periodic systems side by side. Dates and explanations have been omitted from the entries.

Perpetual   **Periodic**

Purchase of 1,000 units at $50 per unit

| Merchandise inventory | 50,000 | Purchases | | 50,000 |
| Accounts payable | | 50,000 | Accounts payable | | 50,000 |

Pay freight of $1,500 for delivery of the purchases

| Merchandise inventory | 1,500 | Freight in | | 1,500 |
| Cash | | 1,500 | Cash | | 1,500 |

Pay for the purchases, taking a 1 percent discount for early payment

Accounts payable	50,000	Accounts payable		50,000
Cash		49,500	Cash		49,500
Merchandise inventory		500	Purchase discounts		500

Sell 500 units for $100 each that cost us $50 each

Accounts receivable	50,000	Accounts receivable	50,000	
Sales		50,000	Sales		50,000
Cost of goods sold	25,000	No entry		
Merchandise inventory		25,000			

Adjusting and Closing Entries

Every company will develop a procedure for recording the transactions that happen every day. Checks will come in, invoices will be sent, and bills will be received, and the company will put in place standard ways of handling these events. Maybe every bill gets recorded as an account payable. Maybe every invoice is recorded as a sale and a receivable. Checks will usually be used to reduce accounts receivable. The standard way in which a company processes these items will depend on the company and the nature and type of transactions it has.

At the end of the accounting period, financial statements will be prepared. As part of this process, the accountant must review the trial balance and ascertain whether adjusting entries are needed. There are five common adjusting entries that companies need to make in order to have their financial statements properly stated:

- Payroll accrual

- Interest expense

- Unearned revenue

- Prepaid expenses

- Prepaid insurance

We will look at each of these entries individually.

Payroll Accrual

Think of your last paycheck. Were you paid for every day you worked right up until the check date? In most companies, the answer is no. There is usually a lag between the end of the payroll period and the pay date (the date of the payroll check). The adjusting entry to accrue the payroll is derived by looking at the portion of the payroll that has not been paid prior to the end of the accounting period. Let's say a company has employees who work only during the week (Monday, Tuesday, Wednesday, Thursday, and Friday). There are three employees, and each of them earns $200 per day (or $1,000 per week). They are paid every other week with a one-week lag. Payday is always Friday. If the last payroll was on December 25, how much should be accrued?

Since we know that December 25 was a Friday (because payday is always Friday) and that there is a one-week lag, so the payroll on December 25 covered the two weeks ending December 18. The following calendar shows the unpaid days in bold type:

M	T	W	Th	F
	1	2	3	4
7	8	9	10	11
14	15	16	17	18
21	**22**	**23**	**24**	**25**
28	**29**	**30**	**31**	

The amount of payroll that should be accrued is therefore calculated as follows:

Number of employees	3
Daily earnings	200
Number of days	9
Total to accrue	5,400

The entry to record this amount is:

12/31/02	Payroll expense	5,400	
	Salaries payable		5,400
	To record accrued payroll		

Along with accruing the payroll, a company will also make an entry to record the payroll taxes associated with the payroll. Let's assume that the payroll taxes are usually about 10 percent of the payroll. An additional entry that is needed is:

12/31/02	Payroll tax expense	540	
	Accrued payroll taxes		540
	To record payroll taxes on accrued payroll		

The next payday will be January 8, 2003. On January 8, we will pay the employees $6,000, calculated as follows:

Number of weeks	2
Work days per week	5
Number of employees	3
Rate per day	200
Total payroll	6,000

It doesn't matter that the payroll on January 8 crosses years. The employees expect two weeks' worth of wages. Separating the payroll between the two years (2002 and 2003) is a job for the accountant making the adjusting entries.

When the company pays the payroll on January 8, the entry is:

01/08/03	Salaries payable	5,400
	Payroll expense	600
	Cash	6,000
	To record payroll	

Only $600 is shown as expense in 2003, which is correct, since the employees worked only one day in 2003 that is included in the payroll of January 8 (the one day of work in this payroll that falls in 2003 is January 1).

Reversing Entries

Reversing entries are an efficient way to make sure that entries that cross periods are always correctly handled. Throughout the year, the company will make the same entry for payroll 25 times:

XX/XX/XX	Payroll expense	6,000
	Cash	6,000
	To record payroll	

However, look at the entry we made on January 8. The first payroll of the year is the one time that the usual entry is not made. Someone in the accounting department has to remember to make the entry a little differently. Reversing entries are a quick and simple way to allow the company to make the usual entry 26 times (meaning every time) and still get the payroll expense into the correct periods.

The reversing entry is the exact opposite of the accrual entry, and it is made on the first day of the next period. The accrual entry made on December 31 was:

```
12/31/02   Payroll expense              5,400
               Salaries payable              5,400
           To record accrued payroll
```

The reversing entry on January 1 (the first day of the next period) is:

```
01/01/03   Salaries payable             5,400
               Payroll expense               5,400
           To reverse accrual entry for payroll
```

After the entry on January 1 is made, Salaries payable is wiped out (the credit of $5,400 is offset by a debit of $5,400), and the Payroll expense account has a credit balance of $5,400. When the standard entry is made on January 8, a debit of $6,000 will be made to the Payroll expense account. The debit of $6,000 and the credit of $5,400 produce a debit balance of $600 in the Payroll expense account, exactly the amount that should show as expense after the first payroll of 2003.

Interest Expense

Interest expense is the cost associated with the use of borrowed money. There may not be a bill received at the end of an accounting period that indicates how much interest expense was incurred during that accounting period. The company will have to compute this amount itself. The general way to compute interest expense is to take the amount of the loan (called the *principal*), multiply it by the interest rate, and then prorate the result for the portion of the year that the amount is outstanding. For example, if a company borrowed $100,000 on July 1 for the term of one year and pays interest at the rate of 10 percent (interest rates are annual amounts unless stated otherwise), how much interest should be accrued at the Balance Sheet date (December 31)?

Principal	100,000
Interest rate	10%
Prorate for time outstanding	50%
Interest to be accrued	5,000

The entry to record the accrued interest is:

12/31/02	Interest expense	5,000	
	Accrued interest payable		5,000
	To record accrued interest		

At such time as the interest is paid, the payable is debited and Cash is credited. If the loan matures on June 30, 2003, the entry to record the payment is:

06/30/03	Loan payable	100,000	A
	Accrued interest payable	5,000	B
	Interest expense	5,000	C
	Cash	110,000	
	To record loan repayment		

A. Recorded when we made the initial entry for the loan:

07/01/02	Cash	100,000	
	Loan payable	100,000	
	To record loan proceeds		

B. From the 12/31/02 entry to accrue interest expense

C. Interest for the period 1/01/03 through 6/30/03

Unearned Revenue

There are times when a customer will prepay for goods or services. In our everyday lives, we do this often—we pay annually for a magazine subscription, for instance. The company cannot record the money as revenue when it is received, since the company still has to provide the goods or services. If a customer prepaid for services in the amount of $10,000, the entry to record the receipt of the money is:

XX/XX/XX	Cash	10,000	
	Unearned revenue	10,000	
	To record receipt of unearned revenue		

At the end of the period, the company has to determine whether any of these goods or services have been provided. If this is a magazine company and the unearned revenue is for subscriptions, the company will count how many issues were sent and make an adjusting entry to remove this amount from Unearned revenue (and move it to Revenue). So, continuing with our example, assume that at year-end the company determines that 40 percent of the prepaid services have been provided. The adjusting entry would be:

12/31/02	Unearned revenue	4,000	
	Revenue		4,000
	To record revenue earned		

Prepaid Expenses

At the end of each period, the company needs to review each item that was recorded as a prepaid expense to determine whether any of this expense has been used up. If so, the company should debit the expense and credit the prepaid expense for the portion used up. The balance remaining in Prepaid expense should represent the amount of expense left to be used.

Closing Entry

After the financial statements have been prepared, the last step in the accounting process is to close the books. This is done with the use of the closing entry. The closing entry takes all the income and expense accounts and makes their balance zero (0). The income and expense accounts are known as *temporary accounts*, since the balance is reset to zero each year. Balance sheet accounts are known as *permanent accounts*, since their balances carry over from year to year.

The temporary accounts are those accounts that are contained on the Income Statement and the Dividend account from the Statement of Retained Earnings. These statements cover a period of time, so the accounts have to be reset to zero so that the next period's transactions can be entered without commingling the transactions for the two periods. The process of making the closing entry is extremely simple: You debit all the accounts with credit balances and credit all the accounts with debit balances. Any amount necessary to balance the entry will be put to Retained earnings. Figure 18-1 gives the Income Statement from Chapter 2.

The entry to close the accounts would be:

FIGURE 18-1

Jeffry Haber Company
Income Statement
For the Year Ended December 31, 2002

Revenues:	
Sales	$250,000
Interest income	500
Total revenue	$250,500
Expenses:	
Payroll	$125,000
Payroll taxes	20,000
Rent	10,000
Telephone	7,000
Office supplies	3,000
Total expenses	$165,000
Net income	$ 85,500

12/31/02	Sales	250,000
	Interest income	500
	Payroll	125,000
	Payroll taxes	20,000
	Rent	10,000
	Telephone	7,000
	Office supplies	3,000
	Retained earnings	85,500
	To close the accounts	

Notice that the amount of the credit to Retained earnings is the same as the net income for the year. The net income was brought to the Statement of Retained Earnings as an increase to the beginning balance. Figure 18-2 shows the Statement of Retained Earnings from Chapter 2.

The entry to close the Dividends account is:

12/31/02	Retained earnings	35,500
	Dividends	35,500
	To close the Dividends account	

FIGURE 18-2

Jeffry Haber Company
Income Statement
For the Year Ended December 31, 2002

Beginning balance, January 1, 2002	$100,000
Add: Net income	85,500
Less: Dividends	35,500
Ending balance, December 31, 2002	$150,000

The beginning balance in the general ledger for Retained earnings was $100,000. During the year, no entries have been made to the Retained earnings account. The financial statements indicate that the balance in Retained earnings should be $150,000 (see both the Statement of Retained Earnings and the Balance Sheet). The closing entries get the Retained earnings account to the correct ending balance of $150,000. In the closing entry for income and expense, we increase Retained earnings by $85,500, and in the entry to close the Dividends account, we reduce Retained earnings by $35,500. The ending balance is $150,000:

Beginning balance	$100,000
Closing entries:	
Increase	85,500
Decrease	35,500
Ending balance	$150,000

The closing entries make the income, expense, and Dividends accounts go to zero and simultaneously get the Retained earnings account balance to the amount shown as the ending balance on both the Statement of Retained Earnings and the Balance Sheet.

19

Specialized Journals

In order to make the operation of the accounting department flow smoothly and efficiently, specialized journals are used. The purpose of the specialized journals is to allow for segregation of duties (so that different people in the department are assigned tasks that do not overlap), to keep details out of the general ledger, and to permit employees to work simultaneously.

Segregation of duties is a key ingredient in the internal control design of an accounting department. Think of a fast-food restaurant—if a bunch of employees are all using the same cash register, can the supervisor blame anyone in particular if the register comes out short? Probably not. That is why it is a good internal control to have one employee responsible for the register—if anything goes wrong with it, management knows whom to hold responsible. Segregation of duties in an accounting department is based on the same idea. When duties are segregated, each person is responsible for a specific task. One person might be responsible for recording the transactions in the Cash account, while someone else actually receives the money for deposit, and yet a third person is responsible for the checks that will come out of the account. Management assigns tasks in such a way that no one employee has access to both the records of an asset and the physical asset.

The balance of every account is maintained in the general ledger. In order to streamline the general ledger and keep it easy to use, it is common to put in less detail and make fewer entries that will clutter it up. It would not be unusual for there to be one monthly posting from each specialized journal to the general ledger. As an example, one of the specialized journals is the sales journal. All of the sales for the month will be listed in the sales journal. The totals from the journal are what will be posted to the general ledger. There might be 100,000 entries in the monthly sales journal, but there will just be one monthly entry in the general ledger.

Each company has only one general ledger. If there were no subsidiary journals, then only one person could work with the general ledger at a time. Having specialized journals allows employees to work simultaneously.

Cash Receipts Journal

The cash receipts journal is used to record the receipt of money (checks and cash) for deposit to the Cash (checking) account. Any item that will result in a debit to the Cash account can be put in the cash receipts journal. The columns generally utilized will include Date, Name/Description, Check Number, Amount, Accounts Receivable (for companies that sell on credit), Sales, and Other.

Let's say that on January 2, 2002, the company received three checks in the mail. The first check is a check from ABC Company in the amount of $1,000 for payment of an invoice. The check number was 3944. The second check was from the DEF Company for $2,500 (check number 1213), also for payment of an invoice. The third check was from the GHI Company for $500 (check number 989) as a prepayment of an order. The cash receipts journal would look like the following:

Date	Name/ Description	Check #	Amount	Accounts Receivable	Other	Acct
1/2/02	ABC Company	3944	1,000	1,000		
1/2/02	DEF Company	1213	2,500	2,500		
1/2/02	GHI Company	989	500		500	UR
Total			4,000	3,500	500	

The entry on January 2, 2002 (assuming that entries are posted daily to the general ledger), would be:

1/2/02	Cash	4,000
	Accounts receivable	3,500
	Unearned revenue	500
	To record cash receipts	

Payments are also individually posted to the subsidiary ledger to keep the customer's account balance up to date and accurate.

Cash Disbursements Journal

The cash disbursements journal is used for any transaction where the credit is to Cash (the checking account). Often, this will be for payments on account (paying vendors that we owe money to—our accounts payable), for prepayments, for rent, for taxes, or for other specialized payments. The columns in the journal will usually include Date, Check Number, Payee, Amount, Accounts Payable, and Other. In addition, any accounts that usually get paid more than once a period will have a dedicated column.

To illustrate, if on January 3 we pay a utility bill in the amount of $540 with check number 134 (the utility company is Con Edison), pay the Acme Office Supply Company for an order we received in the amount of $235 using check number 135, and pay the landlord (XYZ Properties) rent in the amount of $4,500 with check number 136, the entries in the cash disbursements journal will be:

Date	Payee	Check #	Amount	Accounts Payable	Other	Account
1/3/02	Con Edison	134	540	540		
1/3/02	Acme Suppl	135	235	235		
1/3/02	XYZ Prop	136	4,500		4,500	Rent
	Total		5,275	775	4,500	

The entry in the general journal would be (assuming daily posting):

1/3/02	Accounts payable	775	
	Rent expense	4,500	
	Cash		5,275
	To record cash disbursements		

For the payments to Con Edison and ACME Supply, we show the payment in the "Accounts payable" column because an invoice has previously been received and recorded. When the invoice for Con Edison was received, the entry would have been to debit Utility expense 540 and to credit Accounts payable 540 to record the utility invoice.

In contrast, no invoice has been recorded from XYZ Properties, so the Accounts payable column is not used. We record the payment in the related expense account.

Purchases Journal

The purchases journal is used whenever the credit goes to Accounts payable. The usual columns will be for Date, Vendor, Invoice Number, Amount, and whatever types of purchases the company usually makes. This might be Inventory, Office Supplies, Dues and Fees, and, of course, Other. (Every journal should have a column for Other, as trying to anticipate every transaction that can possibly occur usually doesn't work out. The Other column handles infrequent events nicely.)

The following is a typical purchases journal:

Date	Vendor	Invoice #	Amount	Inven-tory	Other	Account
1/02	Staples	12458	145		145	Office supplies
1/02	UVW Merch	3333	750	750		
1/02	Con Edison		540		540	Utilities
1/02	Acme Suppl	2304	235		235	Store supplies
	Total		1,670	750	920	

The entry from the purchases journal would be:

1/02/02	Inventory	750
	Office supplies	145
	Store supplies	235
	Utilities	540
	Accounts payable	1,670
	To record purchases	

Sales Journal

The sales journal is used to record the company's sales. The columns usually include Date, Customer, Description (or reference to a sales order or purchase order), Amount, Sales Amount, Sales Tax, Delivery Charges (if the company ships its products and then charges the customer), and, of course, Other.

Date	Customer	PO	Amount	Sales	Sales Tax	Other	Acct
12/01	ABC Comp	345	1,000	910	90		
12/02	DEF Comp	112	2,500	2,300	200		
12/02	MNO Comp	002	4,000	3,650	350		
	Total		7,500	6,860	640		

The journal entry for these transactions would be:

12/02/01	Accounts receivable	7,500
	Sales	6,860
	Sales tax payable	640
	To record sales	

Payroll Journal

The payroll journal, also called the payroll register, is used to record the payroll for the company. The columns in this journal will include Date, Employee Name, Check Number, Amount, Gross Payroll, and columns for deductions (social security, Medicare, federal withholding, state withholding, city or local withholding, disability withholding, and voluntary withholdings, such as those for health insurance, dental insurance, 401(k), and any other).

Here is a sample payroll register for the December 25 payroll of the Jeffry Haber Company:

Pay date: December 25, 2002
Pay period: December 5–18, 2002

Employee	Gross Wages	Fed W/H	FICA W/H	Med W/H	State W/H	Net Wages
Jones	2,000	200	124	29	50	1,597
Smith	2,000	100	124	29	20	1,717
Doe	2,000	50	124	29	10	1,787
Total	6,000	350	372	87	80	5,101

The entry to record the 12/25/02 payroll from the register is:

12/25/02	Payroll expense	6,000	
	Federal tax withheld		350
	FICA withheld		372
	Medicare withheld		87
	State tax withheld		80
	Cash		5,101
	To record payroll		

When the taxes withheld are remitted to the appropriate government authorities, the entry is a debit to the withholding account (which is a current liability) and a credit to Cash.

CHAPTER 20

Statement of Cash Flows

The fourth statement in a set of financial statements is the Statement of Cash Flows. Preparing the Statement of Cash Flows is not as easy as preparing the other statements. We don't use the trial balance to prepare the Statement of Cash Flows; instead, we have to compute the elements of the statement individually. Preparing this statement is an advanced concept, although I will try to make it simple. The purpose of the statement is to provide information about where cash was generated and what cash was spent on. There are three main sections to the statement:

- Cash flows from operations
- Cash flows from investing activities
- Cash flows from financing activities

Cash flows from operations involve the inflow and outflow of cash in the course of running the business. This involves cash received from customers and cash spent on salaries, inventory, rent, supplies, and other similar items. Add all the cash inflows and subtract all the cash outflows, and the difference is the net cash inflow or outflow from operations.

Cash flows from investing activities involve the cash spent on acquiring assets such as plant, property, and equipment; the cash used to make investments in the stock of other companies; the cash used in making loans; the cash received from the sale of plant, property, and equipment; the receipt of loan payments; and the cash received from the sale of investments. Add all the inflows and subtract all of the outflows, and the difference is the net cash inflow or outflow from investing activities.

Cash flows from financing activities involve the cash received or paid for the issuance of debt (such as bonds, notes, or loans on the cash inflow side and loan payments on the outflow side) and the sale of the company's stock (not the stock of another company). The payment of dividends to shareholders is also a financing cash outflow. Add the cash outflows from financing activities and subtract them from the cash inflows. The difference is the net cash provided by financing activities. (If the cash outflows are greater than the inflows; then the result is net cash used by financing activities.)

When you add the three subtotals together (net cash provided or used by operating activities, investing activities, and financing activities), you get the total cash provided or used. Add this number to or subtract it from the balance of cash at the end of last year and you should get the balance of cash at the end of this year. This is called *articulation*. Articulation is the way one statement relates to another. In this case, taking the three cash flows and adding them to (or subtracting them from) the beginning balance of cash should yield the ending balance of cash that appears on the Balance Sheet. This will also serve as a check that the Statement of Cash Flows has been prepared properly.

There are two acceptable methods of preparing the statement: the direct method and the indirect method. The indirect method is used by the overwhelming majority of companies. It is usually easier to prepare, and the calculations come from readily available figures. By contrast, the information needed for the direct method is not always easy to get. Furthermore, if you do use the direct method, there is an additional step on the cash flow statement—the preparation of a reconciliation that is very similar to the cash flow statement prepared by the indirect method, so when you use the direct method, you actually wind up using both methods. The methods differ in how the cash flow from the operations section is computed. The sections on cash flows from financing and investing are essentially the same in either case.

Direct Method

The direct method provides the information that users really want, such as how much cash was paid by the customers and how much cash was spent on running the business. How would a company get the information about the amount of cash paid by customers? It cannot use sales, because in most circumstances sales are made on credit. It cannot use the credits to the Accounts receivable account, because there are many adjustments that flow through the credit side of Accounts receivable (sales discounts and sales returns, to name a few). In order to provide this information, the accounting system has to be designed with the ability to identify the amount of cash paid by customers, and accounting systems often are not designed that way.

Indirect Method

The indirect method starts with the notion that the information required by the direct method is not available, so there has to be another way to obtain similar information. If the company used the cash basis of accounting, the cash flows provided by operating activities would be net income. Since the company uses the accrual basis, however, revenues are not the same thing as cash inflows, because some revenue may still be owed (it's in Accounts receivable), and expenses are not the same thing as cash outflows, because some expenses may not have been paid for yet (they are in Accounts payable). If we start with net income, is there a way to adjust net income to approximate the cash inflows and outflows? In other words, can we somehow modify the accrual basis Income Statement to get the net cash flow from operating activities?

The indirect method starts with net income, adjusts this figure for any expenses that did not use cash, and then modifies it by using the changes from this year to last year in the current assets and current liabilities sections of the Balance Sheet. That sentence is quite a mouthful. As a beginning student of accounting (whether through school or learning on your own), it is not important to understand why this works. Just know that it does. When you work with it a while, it will become apparent.

The most common noncash expenses are depreciation and amortization. If these appear on the Income Statement, they are added back to net income.

To approximate the cash provided by customers, we start with net income, which contains the sales figure. Let's say Accounts receivable went up from last year. That would imply that a portion of this year's sales has not been collected, and therefore we reduce net income by the amount of the increase in Accounts receivable. If Accounts receivable went down from last year, that would imply that not only did we collect all of this year's sales, but we also collected some of last year's sales. So we would add the decrease in Accounts receivable to net income.

If Accounts payable increased from last year, then a portion of this year's expenses did not require the use of cash. So we adjust for the increase in Accounts payable by adding it to net income. If Accounts payable went down, that would mean that not only did all of this year's expenses involve the use of cash, but we also a paid a portion of the expenses that we owed at the end of last year. We need to subtract the decrease in Accounts payable from net income.

Figure 20-1 shows how the changes in current assets and current liabilities will be used to adjust net income.

The adjustments use this logic: In trying to figure out the change in Cash, in order for Accounts receivable to increase,

FIGURE 20-1	
	Adjustment to Net Income
Current assets	
Increase	−
Decrease	+
Current liabilities	
Increase	+
Decrease	−

we need to debit it. Therefore, we are left with a credit to Cash, which reduces Cash. Thus, an increase in Accounts receivable (or any other current asset) is a reduction to net income in the cash flows from the operating activities section. The opposite holds true as well: In order for Accounts receivable to decrease, it needs to be credited. If we credit Accounts receivable, we are left needing a debit, which increases Cash and hence is a positive adjustment to net income in arriving at operating cash flows.

If Accounts payable went down, then it must have been debited. That means there must have been a credit going to Cash, which yields a reduction of net income. The opposite is true as well: If Accounts payable increased, then it must have been credited. That means that a debit is needed to balance the entry, which increases Cash.

Figure 20-2 is an example of the cash flows from the operating activities section of the Statement of Cash Flows.

FIGURE 20-2

Jeffry Haber Company
Statement of Cash Flows
For the Year Ended December 31, 2002

Operating Activities:	
Net income	$1,000,000
Add:	
Expenses not using cash	
Depreciation	65,000
Increase in accounts receivable	(120,000)
Increase in inventory	(90,000)
Decrease in prepaid expense	35,000
Increase in accounts payable	220,000
Increase in salaries payable	70,000
Decrease in rent payable	(50,000)
Cash provided by operating activities	$1,130,000

Ratio Analysis

The only reason a company prepares financial statements is to provide information to interested users. These users include potential investors, stockholders, bankers, and credit-issuing companies and some government offices. How the outside parties use the information depends on their role and the questions they are trying to answer.

As part of the analysis process, the financial statements are commonly used to prepare ratios. These ratio analyses involve taking some of the numbers on the statements and relating them to other numbers, then making comparisons. Ratios are very useful because they relate different elements of financial information. These relationships provide a tremendous amount of information and allow for both easy tracking of trends over time and simple comparisons among companies. Ratios also have the ability to *normalize* the information. Normalizing means making the data for smaller companies comparable to that for larger companies.

If you were thinking of making an investment in a company (such as by purchasing stock), you might also be considering the competitors of the company you are interested in. You would probably want to invest in the company that had the greatest likelihood of going up in value. Ratio analysis can aid comparability (make it easier to compare companies to other companies).

Other forms of analysis are called *vertical analysis* and *horizontal analysis*. Vertical and horizontal analyses involve comparing the company with itself. We will illustrate the different types of analysis that are commonly done.

Horizontal and Vertical Analysis

Horizontal analysis involves taking the financial statements for a number of years, lining them up in columns, and comparing the changes from year to year. Figure 21-1 shows an example of horizontal analysis.

Vertical analysis involves taking the information on the

FIGURE 21-1					
	2000	**2001**	**Change**	**2002**	**Change**
Revenue	1,000,000	1,200,000	20.0%	1,500,000	25.0%
Salaries	600,000	700,000	16.7%	800,000	14.3%
Rent	110,000	120,000	9.1%	140,000	16.7%
Supplies	65,000	70,000	7.7%	72,000	2.9%
Telephone	50,000	55,000	10.0%	65,000	18.2%
Other	8,000	12,000	50.0%	15,000	25.0%
Net Income	167,000	243,000	45.5%	408,000	67.9%

financial statements and comparing all the numbers to a single number on the statement. For instance, on the Income Statement, all the accounts are expressed as a percentage of sales (or revenue). Figure 21-2 shows an example of vertical analysis.

Ratio Analysis

Ratio analysis is a technique that involves computing some common ratios. These ratios involve comparisons of certain numbers contained in the financial statements. Certain analysts are partial to certain ratios. While there are thousands of possible ratios, there is a core group of common ratios. These are divided into three groups: liquidity ratios, efficiency ratios, and profitability ratios. When two companies are compared, it will often happen that some ratios will favor one company and other ratios will favor the other. You have to take all the ratios together, see how much difference there is, and weigh which ones you will rely on. The choice is largely a matter of personal preference.

	FIGURE 21-2					
	2000	**%**	**2001**	**%**	**2002**	**%**
Revenue	1,000,000	100.0%	1,200,000	100.0%	1,500,000	100.0%
Salaries	600,000	60.0%	700,000	58.3%	800,000	53.3%
Rent	110,000	11.0%	120,000	10.0%	140,000	9.3%
Supplies	65,000	6.5%	70,000	5.8%	72,000	4.8%
Telephone	50,000	5.0%	55,000	4.6%	65,000	4.3%
OTHER	8,000	0.8%	12,000	1.0%	15,000	1.0%
Net Income	167,000	16.7%	243,000	20.3%	408,000	27.2%

Liquidity Ratios

Liquidity ratios measure the ability of a company to generate cash and to pay its obligations when they come due. The following are the most common liquidity ratios:

Working capital (current assets – current liabilities). This is really not a ratio, but a calculation. Calculating working capital will let an analyst know if there are more current assets than current liabilities, and how much more. It is better to have more current assets than current liabilities.

Current ratio (current assets/current liabilities). This ratio relates current assets to current liabilities. For this ratio, bigger is better.

Quick ratio (also called the acid-test ratio) [(cash + accounts receivable + marketable securities)/current liabilities]. Since not all current assets are created equal, the quick ratio omits some current assets. There is no exact way to compute the ratio, but the formulation given here is commonly used. Generally, inventory and prepaid expenses are omitted from the numerator. Bigger is better for this ratio as well.

Efficiency Ratios

Efficiency ratios provide an indication of how well a company is managing its resources. The common efficiency ratios are:

Asset turnover (net sales/average total assets). This ratio provides an indication of how well the assets are being employed in producing sales. Notice that the denominator is average total assets. Generally, when a Balance Sheet item (in this case, total assets) is used in a ratio with a non-

Balance Sheet item (in this case, net sales, which is an Income Statement item), the average value of the Balance Sheet item will be used. To get the average value, take the amount from last year's financial statements and the amount from this year's financial statements, add them together, then divide by 2. For this ratio, bigger is better.

Debt to equity (total liabilities/total equity). This ratio shows how much of the capital in the company was provided by creditors and how much was provided by investors. If this ratio were zero, it would indicate that there was no debt. For this ratio, less is more.

Profitability Ratios

Profitability ratios provide an indication of how well the company is doing at making money.

Profit margin (net income/net sales). This ratio shows what percentage of sales becomes net income. The maximum that this ratio can be is 1, and the closer you get to 1, the better.

Return on assets (net income/average net assets). This ratio shows how much income the assets generated. Whenever you are faced with the issue of whether it is better for a ratio to be larger or smaller, try holding either the numerator or the denominator constant. Let's hold average net assets constant. Now let's vary the numerator (net income). Would we prefer net income to be higher? If so, then we want the numerator to be larger, and given that the denominator is constant, we want the ratio to be higher. Since we are happier with higher net income, which leads to a larger ratio, we can say that bigger is better for this ratio.

Earnings per share [(net income − preferred dividends)/average shares outstanding]. This is a widely reported ratio that allows the net income of companies of different sizes to be compared. For this ratio, bigger is better.

Price/earnings ratio (stock price/earnings per share). This ratio relates the market price of the stock to the earnings available for common shareholders. This ratio is also widely reported. There is no definite way to conclude whether bigger is better, since you would want both the numerator and denominator to be higher.

All of these ratios are summarized in Figure 21-3.

FIGURE 21-3	
Ratio	**Calculation**
Liquidity	
Working capital	Current Assets − Current Liabilities
Current ratio	Current Assets / Current Liabilities
Quick ratio	(Cash + Accounts Receivable + Marketable Securities) / Current Liabilities
Efficiency	
Asset turnover	Net Sales / Average Total Assets
Debt to equity	Total Liabilities / Total Shareholder's Equity
Profitability	
Profit margin	Net Income / Net Sales
Return on assets	Net Income / Average Total Assets
Earnings per share	(Net Income − Preferred Dividends) / Average Common Shares Outstanding
Price/earnings ratio	Market Price of the Stock / Earnings per Share

Summary

So there you have it—the whole of the financial accounting process, from the making of journal entries to the analysis of the company using a variety of analytic techniques. To be sure, for any topic covered, hundreds more pages could be devoted to adding depth to the information, but that is outside the purview of this book. The goal of this book is to provide all the information, techniques, and tips necessary to allow someone who is interested in financial accounting to handle 99 percent of the events that can reasonably be expected to occur.

Glossary

This glossary will define (in brief terms) the technical words that are used in this book. In addition, for any accounts that are defined, there will also be information on the financial statement in which the account can be found and the effect that debits and credits have on the balance of the account. There is also a reference to the chapter in which the defined term is covered. These chapter references are not an index, since many of the words will be used in a number of chapters. The reference points to the chapter in which the term is described and given the most coverage.

The following is the key to the abbreviations used in the glossary:

Stmt	The financial statement(s) in which an account appears
BS	Balance Sheet
IS	Income Statement
RE	Statement of Retained Earnings
CF	Statement of Cash Flows
Debits	The effect debits have on the account

Credits   The effect credits have on the account

Chap   The main chapter in which the word is covered

Incr   The effect will be to increase this account

Decr   The effect will be to decrease this account

The glossary is organized in the following format:

Term Definition	Stmt	Debits	Credits	Chap

Accounting equation   3
The formula Assets = Liabilities + Equity.

Accounts payable   BS   Decr   Incr   14
Amounts owed by the company for goods and services that
have been received, but have not yet been paid for. Usually
Accounts payable involves the receipt of an invoice from the
company providing the services or goods.

Accounts receivable BS   Incr   Decr   7
Amounts owed to the company, generally for sales that it has
made.

Accrued expenses   BS   Decr   Incr   13
payable
Expenses that have to be recorded in order for the financial
statements to be accurate. Accrued expenses usually do not
involve the receipt of an invoice from the company providing
the goods or services.

Accumulated   BS   Decr   Incr   11
depreciation
A contra-fixed asset account representing the portion of the
cost of a fixed asset that has been previously charged to

expense. Each fixed asset account will have its own associated accumulated depreciation account.

Additional paid-in   BS   Decr   Incr   16
capital
Amounts in excess of the par value or stated value that have been paid by the public to acquire stock in the company; synonymous with *capital in excess of par.*

Adjusting entries   18
The entries needed at the end of an accounting period to properly state certain account balances.

Allowance for   BS   Decr   Incr   7
doubtful accounts
A contra account related to accounts receivable that represents the amounts that the company expects will not be collected.

Allowance method   BS   7
A method of adjusting accounts receivable to the amount that is expected to be collected based on company experience.

Articulation
When numbers from different financial statements relate to one another.

Assets   BS   Incr   Decr   5
Items owned by the company or expenses that have been paid for but have not been used up.

Authorized shares   BS   16
The number of shares of stock that the company is legally authorized to sell.

Bad debts   IS   Incr   Decr   7
The amount of accounts receivable that is not expected to be
collected.

Balance Sheet   BS   2
One of the basic financial statements; it lists the assets, liabilities, and equity accounts of the company. The Balance Sheet
is prepared using the balances at the end of a specific day.

Bank reconciliation   6
The process of taking the balances from the bank statement
and the general ledger and making adjustments so that they
agree.

Bonds payable   BS   Decr   Incr   15
Amounts owed by the company that have been formalized by
a legal document called a *bond.*

Building   BS   Incr   Decr   11
The cost of buildings owned by the company.

Capital in excess of BS   Decr   Incr   16
par
Amounts in excess of the par value or stated value that have
been paid by the public to acquire stock in the company; synonymous with *additional paid-in capital.*

Cash   BS   Incr   Decr   6
Amounts held in currency and coin (commonly referred to as
petty cash) and amounts on deposit in financial institutions.

Cash disbursement   19
journal
A journal used to record the transactions that result in a credit
to cash.

Cash receipts   19
journal
A journal used to record the transactions that result in a debit
to cash.

Closing entries   18
The entries that transfer the balances in the revenue, expense,
and dividend accounts to Retained earnings and zero out the
revenue, expense, and dividend accounts for the next period.

Common stock   BS   Decr   Incr   16
Shares of ownership sold to the public.

Contra-asset   BS   Decr   Incr   7
account
An offset to an asset account that reduces the balance of the
asset account.

Contra-equity   BS   Incr   Decr   16
account
An account that reduces an equity account. An example is
Treasury stock.

Contributed capital BS   Decr   Incr   16
The amount put into the business by the owners by purchasing stock and by paying more than the par value for the stock
(additional paid-in capital or capital in excess of par).

Control account   7
An account maintained in the general ledger that holds the
balance without the detail. The detail is maintained in a subsidiary ledger.

Cost of goods sold   IS   Incr   Decr   17
The cost of the items that were sold during the current period.

Credit   3
One side of a journal entry, usually depicted as the right side.

Debit   3
One side of a journal entry, usually depicted as the left side.

Declaration date   16
The date on which the board of directors has declared a dividend.

Declining-balance   11
A method of depreciation.

Depreciation   IS   Incr   Decr   11
expense
An expense account that represents the portion of the cost of an asset that is being charged to expense during the current period.

Direct method   CF   20
A method of preparing the operating section of the Statement of Cash Flows that uses the company's actual cash inflows and cash outflows.

Direct write-off   IS   7
method
A method of adjusting accounts receivable to the amount that is expected to be collected by eliminating the account balances of specific nonpaying customers.

Dividend income   IS   Decr   Incr
Income that a company receives in the form of dividends on stock in other companies that it holds.

Dividends   RE   Incr   Decr   16
Amounts paid to the owners of a company that represent a share of the income of the company.

Equipment   BS   Incr   Decr   11
The cost of equipment owned by the company.

Equity   BS   Decr   Incr   16
Amounts contributed to the company by the owners (contributed capital) plus the residual earnings of the business (retained earnings).

Expenses   IS   Incr   Decr   4
Costs involved in running the company.

First-in, first-out   BS   8
A method of accounting for inventory.

Fixtures   BS   Incr   Decr   11
The cost of fixtures owned by the company.

Furniture   BS   Incr   Decr   11
The cost of furniture owned by the company.

General ledger   3
A book that contains all the accounts of the company and the
balances of those accounts.

Gross profit   IS   17
The result of subtracting cost of goods sold from sales. Synonymous with *gross margin.*

Income Statement   IS   2
One of the basic financial statements; it lists the revenue and
expense accounts of the company. The Income Statement is
prepared for a given period of time.

Indirect method   CF   20
A method of preparing the operating section of the Statement
of Cash Flows that does not use the company's actual cash

inflows and cash outflows, but instead arrives at the net cash
flow by taking net income and adjusting it for noncash expenses and the changes from last year in the current assets
and current liabilities.

Intangible assets   BS   Incr   Decr   12
Assets owned by the company that do not possess physical
substance; they usually take the form of rights and privileges
such as patents, copyrights, and franchises.

Interest income   IS   Decr   Incr
Income that a company receives in the form of interest, usually
as the result of keeping money in interest-bearing accounts at
financial institutions and the lending of money to other companies.

Interest payable   BS   Decr   Incr   18
The amount of interest that is owed but has not been paid at
the end of a period.

Inventory   BS   Incr   Decr   8
The cost of the goods that a company has available for resale.

Issued shares   BS   16
The number of shares that the company has sold to the public.

Journalizing   3
The process of taking a transaction and putting it into a form
that allows it to be recorded in the accounting records.

Land   BS   Incr   Decr   11
The cost of land owned by the company.

Land improvements BS   Incr   Decr   11
The cost of improvements to land owned by the company,
such as fencing and outdoor lighting.

Last-in, first-out   BS   8
A method of accounting for inventory.

Leasehold   BS   Incr   Decr   11
improvements
The cost of improvements made to property that the company
leases.

Liabilities   BS   Decr   Incr   13
Amounts owed by the company.

Liquidity   BS   2
A term that means *nearness to cash*; the closer an asset is to
becoming cash or a liability is to using cash, the more liquid
that asset or liability is.

Loans payable   BS   Decr   Incr   15
Amounts that have been loaned to the company and that it
still owes.

Machinery   BS   Incr   Decr   11
The cost of machinery owned by the company.

Net income   IS   2
The last line of the Income Statement; it represents the
amount that the company earned during a specified period.

No par value stock   BS   16
Stock issued by the company that does not have an arbitrary
value (par value) assigned to it.

Notes payable   BS   Decr   Incr   15
Amounts owed by the company that have been formalized by
a legal document called a *note*.

Notes receivable   BS   Incr   Decr   10
Amounts owed to the company that have been formalized by
a legal agreement called a *note*.

Office expense   IS   Incr   Decr
The amount of expense incurred for the general operation of
an office.

Office supplies   IS   Incr   Decr
The cost of the supplies used in running an office.

Outstanding shares BS   16
The number of shares that are in the hands of the public. The
difference between issued shares and outstanding shares is the
shares held as treasury stock.

Par value   BS   16
An arbitrary value assigned by the company to each share of
stock; it is used in the accounting for the sale of stock and in
some jurisdictions for calculating taxes.

Payment date   16
The date established for the payment of a declared dividend.

Payroll expense   IS   Incr   Decr   18
The amount paid to employees for services rendered; synonymous with *salary expense* and *wage expense.*

Payroll journal   19
A journal used to record the payroll of a company.

Payroll tax expense IS   Incr   Decr   18
The amount of tax associated with salaries that an employer
pays to governments (federal, state, and local).

Payroll taxes   BS   Decr   Incr   15
payable
The amount of payroll taxes owed to the various governments
at the end of a period.

Periodic inventory BS   17
system
An inventory system in which the balance in the Inventory account is adjusted for the units sold only at the end of the period.

Permanent   BS   18
accounts
The accounts found on the Balance Sheet; these account balances are carried forward for the lifetime of the company.

Perpetual inventory BS   17
system
An inventory system in which the balance in the Inventory account is adjusted for the units sold each time a sale is made.

Petty cash   BS   Incr   Decr   6
The amount of currency and coin that a company keeps on hand to pay for small purchases and expenses.

Posting   3
The process of taking journal entries and recording them in the general ledger.

Prepaid expenses   BS   Incr   Decr   9
Expenses that have been paid for but have not yet been used up; examples are prepaid insurance and prepaid rent.

Purchase discounts IS   Decr   Incr   17
A contra account that reduces purchases by the amount of the discounts taken for early payment.

Purchase returns   IS   Decr   Incr   17
A contra account that reduces purchases by the amount of items purchased that were subsequently returned.

Purchases   IS   Incr   Decr   17
Items purchased by the company for the purpose of resale.

Purchases journal   19
A journal used to record the transactions that result in a credit
to accounts payable.

Ratio analysis   21
A method of relating numbers from the various financial statements to one another in order to get meaningful information
for comparison.

Record date   16
The date used to decide which shareholders will receive the
dividend. The owners of the shares at the end of this day are
entitled to the dividend.

Rent expense   IS   Incr   Decr
The amount of expense paid for the use of property.

Retained earnings   BS, RE   Decr   Incr   16
The residual earnings of the company.

Revenue   IS   Decr   Incr   18
Amounts earned by the company from the sale of merchandise
or services; often used interchangeably with the term *sales.*

Reversing entry   IS   18
An entry that is made at the beginning of the current period so
that the systems and procedures do not have to be altered to
allow for previously accrued items.

Salaries payable   BS   Decr   Incr   18
Salaries that are owed but have not been paid at the end of a
period.

Salary expense IS Incr Decr 18
The amount paid to employees for services rendered; synonymous with *payroll expense* and *wage expense.*

Sales IS Decr Incr 18
Amounts earned by the company from the sale of merchandise or services; often used interchangeably with the term *revenue.*

Sales discounts IS Incr Decr 17
A contra account that offsets revenue. It represents the amount of the discounts for early payment allowed on sales.

Sales journal 19
A journal used to record the transactions that result in a credit to sales.

Sales returns IS Incr Decr 17
A contra account that offsets revenue. It represents the amount of sales made that were later returned.

Shareholders' equity BS Decr Incr 16
The total amount of contributed capital and retained earnings; synonymous with *stockholders' equity.*

Specialized journals 19
Journals that are used to aid in segregating duties and making the accounting function efficient.

Specific identification BS 8
A method of accounting for inventory.

Stated value stock BS 16
Stock issued by the company that does not have a par value, but does have a stated value. For accounting purposes, stated value is functionally equivalent to par value.

Statement of Cash   CF   20
Flows
One of the basic financial statements; it lists the cash inflows
and cash outflows of the company, grouped into the categories
of operating activities, financing activities, and investing activities. The Statement of Cash Flows is prepared for a specified
period of time.

Statement of   RE   2
Retained Earnings
One of the basic financial statements; it takes the beginning
balance of retained earnings and adds net income, then subtracts dividends. The Statement of Retained Earnings is prepared for a specified period of time.

Stockholders'   BS   Decr   Incr   16
equity
The total amount of contributed capital and retained earnings;
synonymous with *shareholders' equity.*

Straight-line   IS   11
A method of depreciation.

Subsidiary ledger   7
An accounting record giving the detailed transactions in an
account; the subtotals of the debits and credits are posted to
the control account maintained in the general ledger. It helps
to keep the general ledger free of clutter.

T account   3
The format used for a general ledger page. The name of the
account is put on the top line, and a vertical line is dropped
from the top line (hence the "T"). Debits are recorded on the
left side, and credits are recorded on the right.

Temporary   IS, RE   18
accounts
The accounts found on the Income Statement and the Statement of Retained Earnings; these accounts are reduced to zero
at the end of every accounting period.

Treasury stock   BS   Incr   Decr   16
Shares that were sold to the public but have since been repurchased by the company in the open market. Treasury stock
is deducted from the equity section, and is therefore a contra-
equity account.

Trial balance   3
A listing of all the accounts and their balances on a specified
day.

Unearned revenue   BS   Decr   Incr   13
Money that has been paid by customers for work yet to be
done or goods yet to be provided.

Vehicles   BS   Incr   Decr   11
The cost of transportation equipment owned by the company.

Wage expense   IS   Incr   Decr   18
The amount paid to employees for services rendered; synonymous with *salary expense* and *payroll expense.*

Weighted average   BS   8
A method of accounting for inventory.

Index

CPSIA information can be obtained at www.ICGtesting.com
Printed in the USA
LVOW131215300812

296631LV00003B/148/P